FROM THE PERSONAL TO THE POLITICAL

A Women's Education Workbook

The AONTAS Women's Education Group

Maureen Bassett
Eilish McDonnell
Joanna McMinn
Margaret Martin
Aileen Ryan
Mairéad Wrynn

© AONTAS Women's Education Group, 1991

All rights reserved. Except for brief passages quoted in newspaper, magazine, radio or television reviews, no part of this book may be reproduced in any form or by any means, electronic or mechanical, including photocopying or recording, or by any information storage and retrieval systems without prior permission from the Publishers, except where otherwise stated.

First published in Ireland in 1991 by
Attic Press
44 East Essex Street
Dublin 2

British Library Cataloguing in Publication Data
From the personal to the political : a women's education workbook.
1. Women. Education
I. National Association of Adult Education
376

ISBN 1-85594-023-X

Cover Design: Luly Mason
Cover Photograph: Gillian Buckley
Illustrations: Pauline McGrath
Origination: Attic Press
Printing: The Guernsey Press Co Ltd

FROM THE PERSONAL TO THE POLITICAL

A Women's Education Workbook

The AONTAS Women's Education Group

Contents

Section A: THE WORKBOOK

Introduction

Aim of the workbook

During the 1980s we witnessed the growth of personal development type courses among women but not any corresponding growth in women's activity at a social/political level. We believe that women in Ireland are not treated equally. This is what women's oppression means to us. Oppression is experienced by different women in different ways. Factors such as economic and social background, sexual preference, physical and mental ability affect how we are oppressed. We need to learn more about our own and each other's experience; we need to learn more about how we are oppressed as individuals and as groups; and we need to clarify what changes we want and how we might achieve them. We want to see women build on personal experience to bring about social and political change in Irish society. The workbook encourages this movement from the personal to the political.

Who it is aimed at

The workbook is aimed at experienced facilitators and women wishing to become involved in facilitating adult education for women. The ideas and approaches developed here have a broad application and may be of use to a wide variety of groups.

How it was prepared and tested

We spoke to a number of women's groups about women's education. Health, sexuality and education were most frequently mentioned as areas of interest so we designed material on these topics. We tested this material at a series of one-day workshops held in Belfast, Dublin and Galway. We then revised the material with the help of the workshop facilitators, participants' comments, and our own experience as participants in the workshops. The strength of this method was that it involved a broad group of women both as facilitators and as participants and their observations were invaluable.

We learned that the activities for each topic were like a living creature. They grew and developed within the workshops and within our evaluation meetings afterwards. We hope they will continue to grow and to develop whenever they are used.

The more general material was written by sub-groups from within the AONTAS women's group. After careful reading by each member and a series of editorial meetings the material was then revised and rewritten.

The education model we used and why

We wanted a model to structure our learning and one which would explore our chosen topics from a number of perspectives. We also wanted a model which could be applied to any topic of interest so that women could devise activities for themselves. We want to encourage the development of the curriculum of women's education in this way.

The structure of the topics is based on a model of learning originated by Joanna McMinn and Eilish Rooney. This model builds on women's experience and encourages movement from the personal to the political. Briefly it considers any topic from four perspectives: Experience, Critical thinking, Imagination and Action (see pages 16-18).

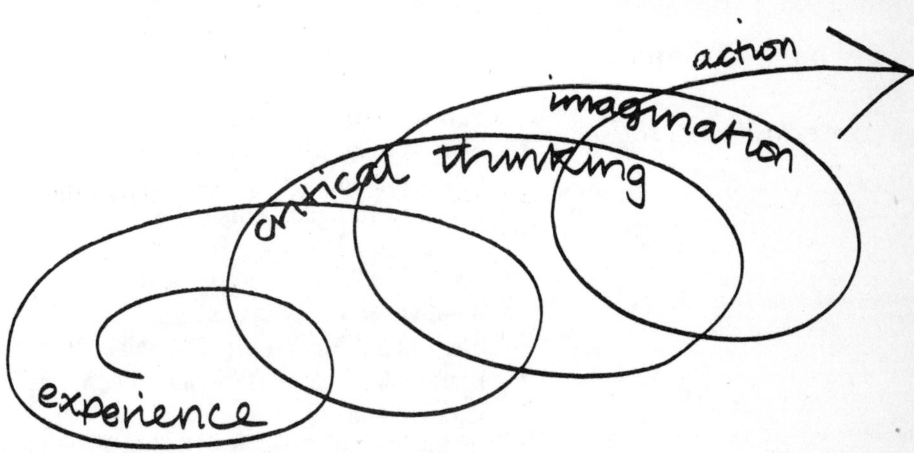

The spiral model of learning

The group's background

The AONTAS Women's Group was established in 1985 and brought together a group of women involved in different ways in women's education as providers, organisers, tutors and students. AONTAS is the National Association of Adult Education. It acts as an umbrella organisation for all those involved in adult educational activities. It aims to promote, develop and support adult education.

At present there are six of us in the group: Maureen Bassett, Eilish McDonnell, Joanna McMinn, Margaret Martin, Aileen Ryan and Mairéad Wrynn. Margaret Martin is a staff member with specific responsibility for women's education. Aileen Ryan was employed on an Social Employment Scheme as a project worker and has been employed on a temporary part-time basis since completing the Scheme. Maureen Bassett and Mairéad Wrynn are members of the AONTAS Executive Committee. Eilish McDonnell and Joanna McMinn are both long-time activists in women's education.

Background to the workbook

We aimed to make contact with women involved in women's education; to establish a network; and to identify key issues and areas of concern. We did this through organising meetings and workshops, and publishing a news sheet. During the 1980s there was a mushrooming of women's and daytime adult education groups but few skilled facilitators were available to work with these groups. Also there was a shortage of training courses on group work skills, particularly outside Dublin.

We wanted to encourage women to share skills and to facilitate groups in their own areas. We brought together a number of women from Dublin, the

Midlands and the West to organise Skills Sharing Workshops. We made links with women's groups in Northern Ireland and organised workshops in conjunction with them with the help of Co-Operation North. The work we were doing excited and enriched us. We wanted to continue. We were on the right track but needed a different approach. The idea of a workbook was born.

Acknowledgements

* Kathleen Forde and Gráinne Healy, former members of the group, who shared their wit and wisdom and made substantial contributions to the development of the workbook.
* The women who facilitated the workshops and generously shared their skills and thoughts: Berni Divilly, Berny McMahon, Mary Kay Mullan, Angela Mulligan, Eilish Rooney and Marie Quiery; and the women who participated in the workshops.
* The AONTAS Executive and Staff who were very supportive during the three years we spent working on the book.
* The Ireland Fund for its financial support.
* Marie Bracken, Offaly and Geraldine Burns, Belfast for their administrative help.
* Jacky Jones, Western Health Board, for organising the workshop in Galway and the Women's Education Project, Belfast for the Belfast workshops.

March 1991

Women's Education

Women's education is concerned with and values women's own experience. It seeks to develop women's self-motivation, self confidence and critical thinking. Women's education is equally fun, sociable, celebratory and good crack.

Through the experience of women's education we have an opportunity to step back and look at the forces operating in our lives. We live in a society in which men and women are encouraged to develop different qualities and to learn different roles in life. Our concerns are often seen as less important than those of men. We are discriminated against in many ways.

Education as we know it generally is made up of packages of knowledge which are neither designed by women nor based on our experience. However, education which focuses on our perspectives can help us become reflective and see how we are viewed as regards our class, age, race, creed, marital status, disability, sexual preference, etc. It can help us revalue our concerns and clarify our needs, wishes and expectations. We can then consider action to initiate change in our lives and in the wider community.

The process

Women's education is concerned with providing a group environment where the process of discovery can be liberating in a safe and relaxed way. For this to happen, certain elements are essential. These include an environment where debate is encouraged, where women engage in discussion and exploration of their lives. It is an environment where information is shared and the process is flowing, noisy and creative. An acceptance of diversity also needs to be recognised and appreciated.

The aim of this process is to awaken our critical faculties, to question our roles and social structures, to challenge accepted norms and to bring our creativity into being.

Working in a group

Women-only groups

While many people recognise the importance of women's education some challenge the idea of women-only groups. Here are some reasons which support and encourage the need for such groups:

* For many of us being in a women's group is the first time we have felt our interests are central and important. In mixed groups male perspectives and interests are usually the focus point and tend to edge out women's views.
* Women's groups provide space where we can learn to be ourselves and drop the stereotypical ways of behaving which our culture has imposed on us.
* Women's groups give us a chance to explore our leadership skills and potential and to explore different ways of organising and working. In mixed groups men usually adopt positions of leadership as they are used to this in society.
* We need opportunities to become confident in our opinions and speak up. Research has shown that men dominate discussion in mixed groups and frequently interrupt girls and women.
* We need women's groups where we can explore our experience as it is, rather than as we have been told it ought to be.

The Spiral Model of Learning

Originated by Joanna McMinn and Eilish Rooney

Backgound

This model originated in a course which Joanna McMinn and Eilish Rooney developed for the extra-mural programme in the University of Ulster. The programme, *Women Working for Women*, aimed to relate the issues and problems affecting women in their local communities to an analysis of the position of women in society.

As we began to plan the course we asked ourselves a question: how had we learned about ourselves as women in this society?

* We had learned, often the hard way, from our own experience.
* From feminism we had learned a way of analysing and understanding that experience.
* We had also gained from literature, films and plays an imaginative insight into our experience and that of other women.

The ways we had learned then were:

* through our lived **experience**
* from our own and other women's **critical thinking**
* from use of **imagination** in poetry, plays, fiction etc.

From these three different ways of looking at our lives we decided what **action** we wanted to take.

We set ourselves the task of using what we knew about our own learning to inform the structure of the course we were planning. We drew in other tutors who were interested in our approach, and developed a process

> *of drawing on the individual's experience and using imagination to reach beyond the individual experience to an overview of a particular topic. This kind of approach stimulated involvement, thinking, and discussion.**

* Eilish Rooney, 'Women Working for Women', Women's Studies International Forum. (Ailbhe Smyth, Editor, Women's Studies International Forum 1988, Special Issue. *Feminism in Ireland*. Vol 11, No 4, Pergamon Press, Oxford, England 1988)

Personal and political

Within the privacy of our own homes and local groups, we can be powerful and make decisions. Other times we experience conflict and feel controlled. In the public world it is hard to see where women have power. The structures of society seem to work against us and put us in a double bind. There is little reward for staying within the private personal world, or for taking our place in the public political sphere. By providing a model for each topic included in the workbook, our objective is to provide a framework within which women's education groups can explore both the personal and political aspects of their lives as women.

We have designed activities that:

* reflect on our own lived **experience**
* pose questions which encourage **critical thinking** and offer women opportunities to develop their own feminist perspectives
* explore **imaginative** expression of the politics of being a woman in art, films, books etc
* identify personal and collective **action.**

The spiral model

The model is represented as a spiral moving forward.

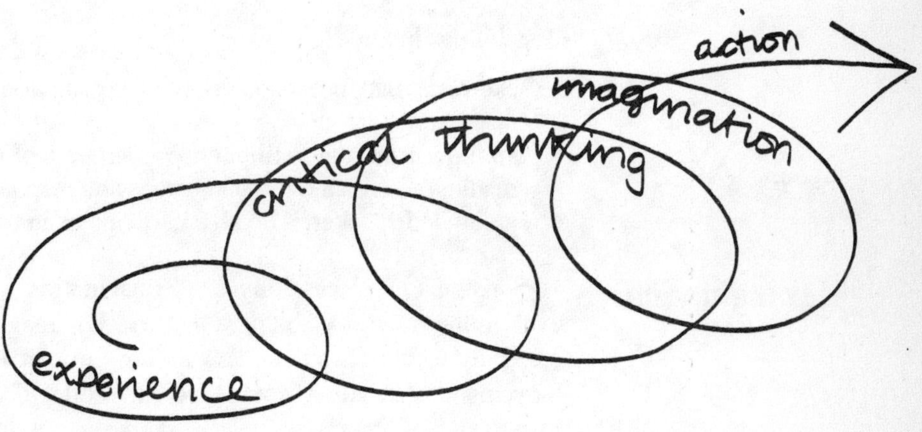

The spiral model of learning

The spiral model of learning creates possibilities to explore learning. Its purpose is to move from experience through critical thinking and imagination into action. It is a flexible structure and is designed to respond to the varied and changing interests of groups.

We learned that in practice, experience, critical thinking and imagination often overlap. Members of a group may want and need to focus on one specific area, for example their own experience.

Flexibility is required in order to create and maintain a balance within the overall framework of a course or workshop. It is crucial to work at the pace of the group.

Experience

Women's experience is the starting point of this model. By experience we mean the personal knowledge gained through living in the world as a girl and as a woman. Each topic contains exercises and activities that facilitate a discussion of women's experience of health, education and sexuality. These form the groundwork validating women's own experience which may well have been ignored, neglected or dismissed in the past. Sharing and discussing that experience with other women encourages solidarity which when achieved can allow for differences to be addressed and conflicts confronted.

Critical thinking

In order to place our experiences in a wider context, ways of analysing and exploring the social, economic and political aspects of our experience are suggested. Critical thinking is a process of exposing and assessing *assumptions* and *facts* about women's roles. A feminist perspective challenges these *assumptions* and *facts* and argues that education, sexuality and health are all experienced by women in ways that have political implications.

Possibilities include:

* exercises that propose different explanations of women's experience for discussion
* an input from the facilitator, or members of the group, based on their own reading, to which everyone listens and responds
* an invited speaker, who also participates in a group discussion.

Imagination

Feminists have successfully used imagination in poetry, plays and fiction to explore the politics of being a woman. By imagination we mean the power of creativity to enrich our understanding through images, language, sounds and movement. Activities could include collage, games, fantasies, films and readings of women's written work. Users of the workbook will be able to contribute their own materials or suggest other ideas.

Action

As we move from the personal to the political, using the dynamics of experience, critical thinking and imagination, energy is released. For this energy to be productive, it is important that space be made for women to decide what action they want to take as a result of their learning. By action we mean steps or measures which contribute to change. This action may be personal, collective or communal, or all three. Structured activities are included to facilitate the action plans that women may wish to make.

Section B: GROUP DYNAMICS

How Groups Work

Introduction

This chapter deals with different aspects of working with groups. The ideas and approaches developed here have a broad application and may be of use to a wide variety of groups. Please read it carefully before preparing your programme.

Section B:

* highlights some aspects of group dynamics and group development;
* outlines how to plan a course;
* provides guidelines for handling the first session with particular emphasis on establishing expectations and ground rules;
* deals with the need for ongoing evaluation and suggests methods for dealing with this.

Throughout the workbook we use the term *facilitator*. The person who fulfils this role is variously described as facilitator, tutor, teacher or group leader. We have used facilitator as it means to *make easy*. Group dynamics can be defined as the process of change which occurs through the interaction of group members.

Learning through and in groups

We are all members of groups throughout our lives. Our social learning is done in groups. Early experiences within the groups to which we have belonged, have a bearing on our behaviour and on our attitudes to groups and to individuals within groups.

Individual behaviour within groups

Membership of groups is a normal part of our lives, yet we often overlook the dynamics existing within groups. When things go wrong we tend to blame other members of the group, withdraw mentally, or perhaps leave the group. When things are going our way, however, we do not always appreciate the part others play in this.

A group that works well provides a base from which the individual can develop her potential and skills. The well-being of a group depends on the healthy functioning of each member, so members and groups are interdependent.

Working in groups

Goals

The goals of an education group may be to learn a new skill, to develop confidence, to improve communication skills, to do creative writing or to pursue a women's studies course — among others.

Rights and responsibilities

Members have basic rights in any group.

The right to know

This can include the right to having information available on methods, planning processes and goals. It is the facilitator's responsibility to provide this information when asked. It is important to use language that is simple and clear.

The right to privacy

It is important that group members are helped to clarify what they are comfortable about disclosing. Emphasise that no one is obliged to jump in with personal disclosures just because someone else has bared her soul. Every woman has the right to withhold information about herself, and has the right to expect others to respect confidentiality. It is essential that an agreement be made by each member of the group that all that happens within the group is confidential. It is the facilitator's responsibility to make sure that this issue is discussed by everyone (see Ground rules handout, page 33).

The right to respect

Every member of a group has the right to be treated with respect as equal, intelligent, capable and different.

Co-facilitation

As facilitator it is your reponsibility to be aware of your limitations, to ensure you are not working in isolation and that you have access to support both for yourself and group members if required. One way of finding support for yourself is to co-facilitate. Co-facilitation helps to ensure that responsibility is shared, makes it easier to review progress, to handle criticism and to do peer evaluation. New ideas and approaches are often triggered.

Some of the elements of co-facilitation are:

* **Listening**: the person not leading a session performs an invaluable role as listener. Since she is not required to participate she can observe what her co-facilitator is doing and how the group members are reacting.
* **Explication**: the person not leading a session can make an input (openly at the time or later) that sheds light, explains, or highlights something that is going on and needs to be acknowledged.
* **Support**: this involves looking out for her co-facilitator during the session.
* **Role modelling**: women in a group observe the team work and behaviour of the co-facilitators and learn from it.

Hidden agendas

Group members may be unclear about what they need and expect from a group when they first join. They come with expectations of the group, of the facilitator and of themselves. Some of the expectations will be in the form of *hidden agendas*. A hidden agenda is a need or expectation that is not made clear within the group. If expectations are not declared they will emerge in one form or another. Spend time early on bringing them into the open (see Activity — hopes, worries and expectations, page 34). In practice, a demand that the group be agreeable and *nice* may cover up a need to avoid disagreement or conflict. Similiarly a demand *for an expert* may cover up a hidden request for answers to individual problems. Some of the hidden agendas remain hidden in spite of the facilitator's skills. The extent to which people are prepared to articulate their needs will depend also on their confidence and experience.

Clarifying expectations, limits and boundaries

In every group expectations are determined by past experiences, individual limitations or fantasy. It is important that attention be drawn to your limits. These might be:

I'm prepared to provide a structure of learning but not to guarantee the outcome.
I'm prepared to listen to your experiences and learn from them but not to give instant solutions.
I'm prepared to cover these items — listing them — but not to give a lecture on psychology, for example.
I'm prepared to deal with conflict but with your support and determination to make things work.

It is important that you are clear about your own limits, ie what you are not prepared to do and make clear your boundaries, ie the extent of your responsibility for the group's learning. Participants will have their own limits too, but may not be aware of them. Groups need clarity right from the beginning — this goes some way to avoiding later recriminations.

Go back to the list of expectations and have another look at them. Clarify whether the group has a shared understanding of what is meant by stated expectations — these often include hidden agendas and demands.

I want the group to share may mean *I want everbody to bare their soul as I do.*
I want to group to be supportive may mean *I want you to listen to me all the time.*
I don't want any rows may mean *I don't want arguments or disagreements* or *group members should always support one another even when they disagree.*

Central to group development and learning is the ability to listen to other viewpoints and express disagreement if necessary. If disagreement is stifled because of some unspoken rule, then learning and change are unlikely to happen.

To help clarify expectations and identify hidden agendas here are some questions you might ask:

* What does support mean to you?
* Does everybody agree with this definition?
* What does confidentiality mean?
* Would you like to be able to disagree?
* How would you stop yourself from saying you disagree?

Be aware that as the course progresses, hopes, expectations and worries may change.

A number of factors shape how the group works. These include stage of development, time limits, level of commitment, motivation, and the resources and support available. Also, each woman will have personal limitations, eg lack of finance, shyness, lack of confidence, priorities and prejudices. Sometimes a member may leave the group without giving a reason. This may be due to one or a number of the factors mentioned above. Whilst you may be able to support her, your limitation may be that you do not have appropriate skills; your boundary will be that this course is not the appropriate place for individual in-depth work. In these cases you may need to encourage women to look for help outside the group. *The Irish Women's Diary and Guide Book* and *Woman to Woman* are useful references.

Stages of group development

Stages of development can be divided into three:

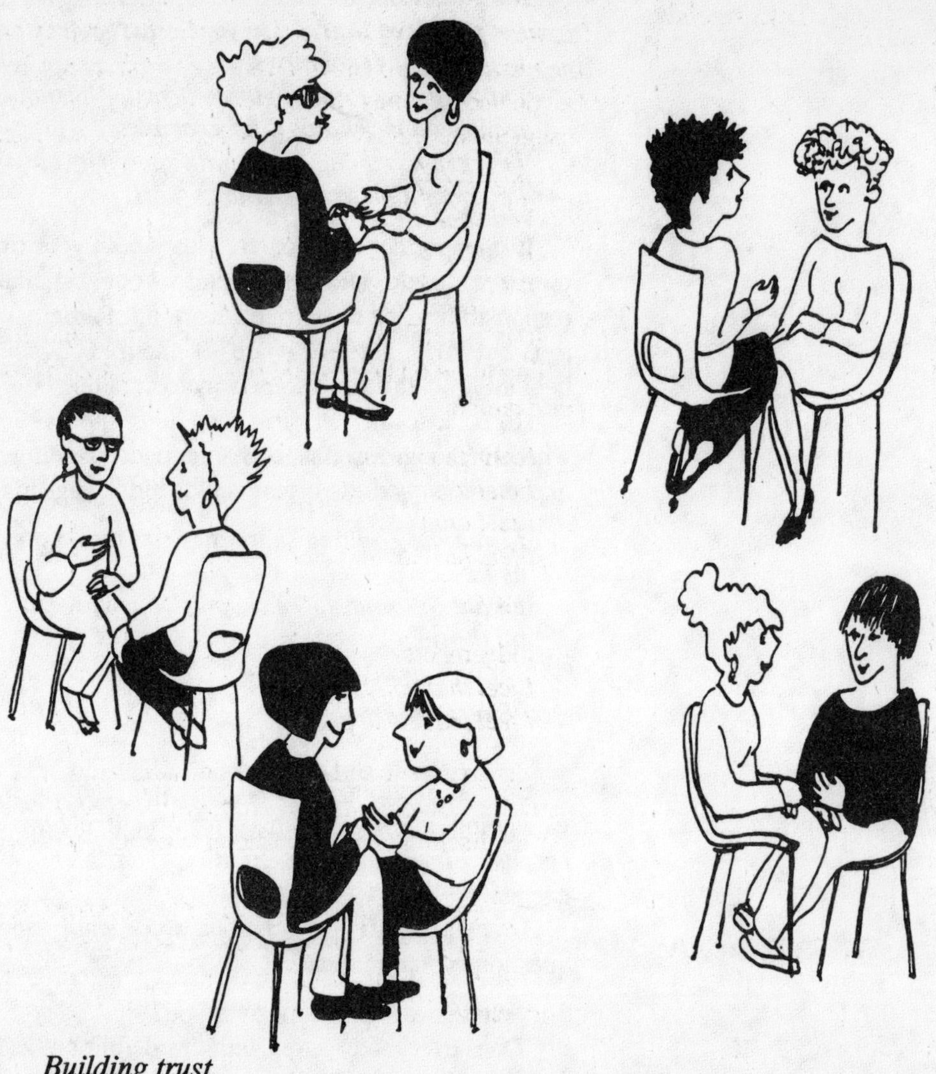

Building trust

Stage 1 Building trust

At this stage group members can be gentle, helpful, eager; careful not to rock the boat, not to disagree, to challenge or to confront unrealistic expectations. They may be anxious about *Will I be accepted? Will I cope? Who are my friends?* One of your tasks will be to create an environment in which these anxieties are acknowledged and in which women can work together.

In Stage 1 women get to know each other and begin to work together, so a *nice* secure feeling is established. However, once women gain confidence it should be possible to air disagreements and differences.

It is important in Stage 1 to structure exercises to contribute to group development. In the beginning women may prefer to work in pairs or small groups. This enables the shyer, less confident women to feel less reluctant to contribute and eventually participate in the large group.

Stage 2
Taking risks

During the first stage an atmosphere of trust is established. Women may now be secure enough to question, disagree, confront and ask for clarification. However, fear of conflict and confrontation may encourage women to maintain the *niceness* at all costs. Disagreement may not be recognised or stated. It may be denied. It may be buried by talking rapidly, by avoiding response to disagreement or by constant use of phrases such as:

Everybody says ....
You should ....
We must all ....
It's the accepted wisdom ....

It is natural to agree on some things and disagree on others. If we are willing to be ourselves and begin with *I* statements disagreements can be aired, for example

feelings expressed
I feel annoyed ....
I feel angry ....
I feel hurt ....

not

judgements
I feel that you ....
I feel that some people ....

Disagreement and conflict are as healthy and natural as harmony and co-operation. Avoidance of conflict in groups is often more damaging than conflict itself. Burying conflict is wasting energy and is time consuming.

Stage 3
Working together

When a group can acknowledge differences and move on, it can be said to have entered Stage 3, ie co-operation. Co-operation means working together towards the same end. It does not involve burying conflict or smoothing over differences.

Group Roles and Group Dynamics

Roles

The behaviour of the group is visible in the roles that people adopt. Some of the roles which emerge will be:

listener	stimulator
questionner	challenger
pacifier	mediator
time-keeper	adviser
risk taker	clarifier
supporter	joker
information giver	gossip
informer	underminer
victim	persecutor
time-watcher	anecdote teller
cynic	attention seeker

Good and *bad* roles can be interchangeable depending on what is happening in the group at the time. For example, listening may not always be the most constructive response. On the other hand, providing information by bringing relevant details into the group can be very constructive.

Dynamics

The dynamics of a group are the active processes at work within it. These processes are visible in the behaviour of the group and the roles people adopt. They begin in the feelings of group members and are developed through complicated interactions which are not always intentional or fully recognised. The dynamics at work include: communication, interaction, and the formation of sub-groups.

If you want to consider the level and quality of communication and interaction present in a group you might want to look for the following and to note the patterns of behaviour:

* Does one woman (or a number) rush in to *help* and smooth over when disagreement and conflict occur?
* How many women speak during the session?
* Is it the same women who are always quiet?
* Do women listen to each other and then reply or do they interrupt?
* How do women sit in the room — lines, circles, close together, at a distance from each other?
* Do women tend to talk to the facilitator or do they develop discussion amongst themselves, looking at and speaking directly to each other?
* What happens at coffee break? Does the group largely stay together or break into small groups? Is anyone left out? What do you do during this break?
* How do women come into/leave the session — early, on time, late, singly or in groups, silently or talking with each other?
* What sorts of gestures/movements do women make, particularly for emphasis of a point or to include/exclude others? Are some more emphatic than others? How much is this personal style, and how much is it a group process?
* Is there conflict or confrontation in the group during this session? Is it dealt with? If so, how? What part do you play?

Guidelines to explore the dynamics within a group

It is vital that discussion of dynamics takes place in an open, exploring way. The objective is to make all group members take active responsibility for their contribution to the group. Begin by establishing ground rules for this discussion. Refer to the ground rule sheet and bring the following to the group's attention:

* Everyone should speak directly out of their own experience in the group. *Everyone knows ....* is not your own experience.
* Feelings should be articulated as *I feel ....* and statement of feeling (one word), eg *I feel irritated*.
* Judgements should be actively discouraged. Judgements often operate under the guise of feelings. Often a clear indication that judgements are being made is when the word *that* comes after I feel, eg *I feel that you are wrong*, as distinct from *I feel uncomfortable, I feel unconfident, I feel*

angry/annoyed. To get clarity ask people to say one word only after *I feel*. Indeed quite often the key word *that* is implied, eg *I feel you're unreasonable* ie *that you're unreasonable* or *I feel you're wrong* ie *that you're wrong*.

* Interactions or questions should be for clarification or extension, not confrontation, eg *You seem to be feeling* .... or .... *I think you are saying* ....

Never underestimate the extent of feelings women bring into a group. They may not be fully aware of these themselves. Such hidden or half recognised feelings are very important in determining what happens in a group. When strong feelings are not expressed, conflict and hostility can result. These feelings may have nothing to do with what is happening in the group. Often they stem from domestic or family concerns, lack of confidence or feelings of inferiority. Often allowing space to *name* them is sufficient. This can be done routinely in an opening circle (see Preparing a session, page 30).

Helpful questions

You may find it useful to display one or some of these questions on a chart.

In this group:

* Do we value and respect each other? (This isn't necessarily the same as liking each other.)
* How do I learn? From whom?
* When does learning take place?
* What kinds of creative/destructive contributions have I made?
* How much have I talked?
* How well have I listened?
* Where is the leadership? Does it pass round the group?
* What have I contributed to the leadership of this group?
* How have I encouraged/discouraged others?
* How have I been encouraged/discouraged by others?
* What is my individual responsibility as a member of this group for my own and other people's learning?
* Do we as a group take collective responsibility for our own learning? What does this involve?
* Let's reconsider our expectations and ground rules — are these being observed?

Body language indicators

Non-verbal language reveals some of the dynamics operating within the group. Observe the group.

Are some members:

* making good eye contact
* nodding in agreement
* being attentive and alert
* digging their heels in — literally
* standing apart
* withdrawing physically — moving a chair, turning aside

* visibly stopping what they are about to say, covering mouth, swallowing back
* becoming pale, blushing
* burying themselves in notes, books, busy behaviour?

Note your interpretations.

Issues of leadership and authority

Within mainstream adult education, one person is understood to be the *leader*, namely the facilitator. However, each woman in a group can take on a leadership role at times. Try to ensure that leadership is shared. It is important that all women realise their potential for leadership without dominating the group. Leadership for women also includes taking their own authority and taking responsibility for contributing to the group. Taking their own authority can include: making clear statements, challenging what they disagree with, or requesting change.

To develop leadership potential:

* encourage quieter women to speak often and freely
* encourage the more fluent and articulate ones to wait their turn
* discourage the *speaking for others* pattern, eg *we all know ....* or *Mary here thinks/feels ....*
* help the group to identify and use the different skills of members, eg
    - organise a guest speaker
    - prepare a poster/publicity
    - record small group discussion
    - participate in role-play
    - collect fees
    - organise practical matters
    - prepare a 10 minute input

All of the above would be less threatening when done jointly.

Real learning is an active process. It happens when we are aware of how we operate in a group while acquiring information, knowledge, and skills. Therefore taking time out (a full or half session) to look at group behaviour can contribute considerably to the development of individuals and of the group.

Planning and Preparation

The success of a course depends on careful planning and thorough preparation. Here we focus on the groundwork which must be done before the course begins. Preparing a session and your first session are dealt with later on.

Planning ahead

If you intend working on a particular topic do some general reading around it — see resource list at the end of each topic. Friends are often a good source of books, ideas and support. Local libraries can be very useful — a good starting point would be to go to the non-fiction section Dewey Ref. 306.

Points to consider before designing a programme:

* What are the interests, needs, and previous experience of your group?
* What is it that you want to do? — objectives
* What will help you? How will you use this?
* What will hinder you? How will you deal with this?
* How will you begin?
* Do you have someone to work with?
* What other help/resources do you think you will need?

Group size

It is a good idea to set limits on the size of a group — min 8-10 and max 10-15. Set a maximum number in advance. If more are interested, you could set up a waiting list, or start a parallel group.

Venue

A suitable venue is essential. Begin by contacting the Adult Education Organiser who is employed by the local Vocational Education Committee. S/he may be able to help with premises. If you prefer to be independent, contact school principals, community councils, clergy/religious, health centre, librarian, or even your local pub.

* Find somewhere bright and comfortable.
* Make sure you won't be interrupted.
* Make sure the room is available every week at the agreed time.
* Organise coffee/tea breaks and crèche facilities.

Designing a programme

The material in this workbook is designed in a sequence of steps. Each topic follows a pattern — experience, critical thinking, imagination and action. You can pick and choose from the suggested material, and/or supplement it with other material drawn from your own resources, depending on the interests of your group.

Questions for designing a programme

* How long will your course be (one day, weekend, term)?
* What will be covered?
* What will not be covered?
* What methods will you use? — see pages 40-46.

Preparing a session

Being well prepared is essential. We have laid out the material for each topic in a sequence of steps. The following elements should also be included in each session:

* **Opening Circle**: eg each woman says briefly how she is — it can be just one word to describe how she is feeling right then. This is useful because if something is happening for a woman, it may get in the way for her or for others.
* **Unfinished business:** ask if there is any unfinished business from the last session, eg *any thoughts on .... during the week, anything you would have liked to say but didn't ....*
* **Introduction**: explain what it is you hope to do in the session and introduce the topic briefly.
* **Activities:** continue with your activities on your chosen topic interspersed as appropriate with icebreakers, games, relaxation exercises etc.
* **Closing circle**: eg a brief verbal evaluation, and/or a word to describe how each woman is feeling right then.

Hints

* Keep it simple.
* Get participants to do the work.
* Be clear about timing (it often takes longer than you might think).
* Be clear about what you want as a result of the activities.
* Make the activities real.

Pacing/Timing

As with good comedy, pacing and timing are the essence of good women's education practice. When planning a session, take into account the number of women in the group and their previous experience. If all of this is very new to most of them, you will need to move slowly. Intersperse activities with trust building exercises, icebreakers, games etc, to facilitate the process of *getting comfortable* with each other.

The nitty gritty

Write out a detailed programme for yourself in advance:

* Prepare your introduction.
* Choose a series of activities.
* Select appropriate icebreakers/games.
* Make a note of reminders for participants, eg to bring along any necessary material for the next session.
* Plan a closing circle.
* List the extras you need, eg scissors, magazines for collage, dice for games, paper for flip chart, bluetack etc. Make a check list.

It is a good idea to prepare additional exercises for each session and to have them ready in case you need them. Feeling prepared can be a source of comfort.

The First Session

This workbook focuses on active learning rather than on passive listening. This may be a new experience for many in your group. Participants might need to be reassured about the approaches used. For example, the opening circle, working in pairs, icebreakers etc, may be intimidating. Go gently.

Additional elements are required in a first session. So along with the opening circle, introduction, activity and closing circle, there needs to be some explanation of the way you work, ground rules, acknowledgement of hopes, worries and expectations, and any housekeeping arrangements that have to be made.

Particularly for the first session it is important to:

* be there well before the first woman arrives
* have the room ready, ie chairs in a circle with extra chairs for unexpected participants or late arrivals
* greet each woman as she arrives
* welcome latecomers too.

Opening circle

Introduce yourself briefly to the group. Ask participants to say their names.

Opening circle

Explanations

Explain how you like to work. You could say something like this: *We are sitting in a circle because it allows us to communicate more directly. It also helps to establish the equality of all members of the group, which includes the 'teacher'. All of us will learn from each other and share experiences and knowledge.* You might ask for comments here. Give an outline of your programme for the session or the course as appropriate. Go on to explain that active learning methods will be used, and give an example from your programme for that session or the example of working in small groups.

Ground rules

The type of women's education suggested in this workbook is based on starting with women's experience and may involve self-disclosure. A clear agreement about issues of confidentiality should be made, ie a verbal agreement from everyone in the room. Some other basic ground rules should be established, eg respect difference, equal time — equal space, etc (see Ground rules handout, page 36).

Housekeeping

You may need to refer to housekeeping arrangements here:

* starting and finishing times
* smoking
* breaks
* responsibility for provision of refreshments
* deadlines for payments (if applicable)
* child care arrangements.

Activity — Hopes, worries and expectation

Explain what it is you hope to do in the activity and introduce it briefly. Ask each woman to introduce herself to one other woman (preferably someone she does not know) and to say something about why she has come on the course. Next, ask participants to move into groups of four. List the following questions on flip chart and ask the groups to discuss:

* What are you hoping for?
* What are you worried about?
* What do you expect of the facilitator?
* What do you expect of the course?

It might be useful to get each participant to write her answers to these questions. (Note: be aware that literacy difficulties might exist.) This activity may be shortened if time is limited.

Feedback

In the large group ask participants to share what they have discussed and record their comments under the different headings. These could be kept as a reference for later. It is important to write up the actual comments and not your interpretation of them. Check that expectations are realistic. Be clear about what the course can and cannot offer.

Some further discussion should be encouraged about what is to be learned and how learning will be done. It is important to allow each woman time to speak in this first session.

Closing circle

Ask for a brief verbal evaluation or a word from each woman about the session.

Troubleshooting

* What will I do if nobody talks? Think about this beforehand, eg be ready to divide the group into twos or threes to facilitate sharing initially. If you prefer you might do a brainstorm just to get thoughts flowing.
* What if they seem giddy? Ask the group if this is so. Then depending on what comes up you might choose to play a game (to physically move them around) or do a relaxation exercise (to help them focus).
* What will I do if we get through the material too quickly? Have additional material on standby, or use the remaining time as the group wishes or even finish a wee bit early — it's not a crime!
* What will I do if the discussion gets heated? Try to clarify what is being debated. Ask each woman involved to state her view and request that she speaks only in the first person. Ensure no one is interrupted. Get the others to say what they have heard. It may be that they have to agree to differ. Refer to the ground rules, ie respect difference, listen, equal time — equal space etc.

Ground Rules Handout

1. **Confidentiality**: agree that personal details and disclosures are not discussed outside the group. You can talk about yourself, your learning and the course content.

2. **Respect difference**: you have the right to be different as do all members of the group.

3. **No interrupting**: give each other time to clarify thoughts and articulate them. Wait until the other is finished before speaking.

4. **Equal time — equal space**: take responsibility for how often you speak in the group and for allowing others equal time and space.

5. **No advice**: come to your own decisions/conclusions about what is right and appropriate for you. Speak from your own experience and do not give advice to others, eg *If I were you I would .... You should ....*

6. **Listen**: pay close attention to what each woman is actually saying, rather than what you want to hear said.

7. **Speak in the first person**: speak directly out of your own experience and use *I* or *I feel* rather than *everybody says* or *most people feel.*

8. **Responsibility**: take responsibility for what you think, do, say and feel in each session. Equally take responsibility for what you do not say in each session.

9. **Disclosure**: only say what you are comfortable with, no matter what others disclose.

Permission to photocopy

Evaluation

From the outset it is important to have a clear idea of the need for ongoing evaluation and how this will be included as part of your work.

Aims of evaluation

The aims of evaluation are to:

* help the group assess how it is developing
* see if expectations have been met
* identify exercises, materials, methods which are useful and those which are not
* identify difficulties or gaps early on
* plan for the future
* discover the facilitator's training needs for this and other work.

To assist the evaluation process details of the group's hopes, expectations and worries need to be recorded. A variety of methods can be used for evaluation both verbal and written. It is important to detail the purposes of evaluation as outlined above. Reinforce the idea that you are also in a learning situation and criticism, as long as it is constructive, can be a powerful factor in enabling you to learn and to change. Encourage participants to be specific rather than general in their comments.

Types of evaluation

A brief verbal evaluation at the end of each session is useful in developing confidence and critical skills informally. For example, a quick round at the end of a session allows women space to say how they are and to mention any unfinished business. It tells each woman how the others are feeling and it helps to keep the focus on the needs of the group.

Some questions on group development, verbal or written, might be:

I came to this session feeling ....
I went away at the end of last week thinking ....
In this course I have got ....
In this course I have not got ....

Some examples of questions on course content:

* What did you like about this session?
* What did you not like?
* Did you get what you wanted?
* How could the activity/session/course be improved?
* If you were planning the course again, would you include this session? Would you have the guest speaker back?
* How would you have liked to change the session?

Sheets could be circulated so that a written record can be kept.

Using the evaluation

The facilitator needs to acknowledge the comments, ideas and interests expressed by the group through the evaluation process. Some of these ideas may be incorporated into your ongoing planning if appropriate. This may involve:

* arriving at agreement on priorities, not necessarily taking the most popular topics only
* pointing out an imbalance on the course, eg some perspectives not getting attention
* suggesting other courses/groups in which interests can be developed, or networks which can be linked into
* devising methods, eg projects, small group discussions etc, where specific needs are addressed.

Section C: ACTIVE LEARNING

Methods

Introduction

At the core of this workbook is the belief that an active approach to learning is most valuable. This approach puts particular emphasis on the experience, knowledge and skills which exist within any group. In this chapter we describe a wide range of active learning methods.

Group discussion

Encourage all women to participate. Give all members of the group an opportunity to speak. Stress the importance of active listening. Allow silences and time for thought. Encourage women to make their own connections and to come to their own conclusions.

Working in sub-groups

Women are sometimes reluctant to participate in large groups and may be more relaxed in a smaller group. Working in sub-groups gives more individual space, increases involvement and saves time.

Break into twos, threes or fours as appropriate. Give a specific amount of time to allow the groups to proceed with the discussion or task. If desirable, report back to the larger group to share ideas or conclusions either verbally or in writing.

When breaking into sub-groups these are some options:

* self-selection
* facilitator allocates a number to each participant depending on the number of sub-groups she wishes to have or the size of the large group. For four groups, she begins on her left, numbering each participant 1, 2, 3 or 4, and repeating around the group. Then she asks all 1s to work together, all the 2s to work together, etc
* ask women to work with someone they have not worked with before.

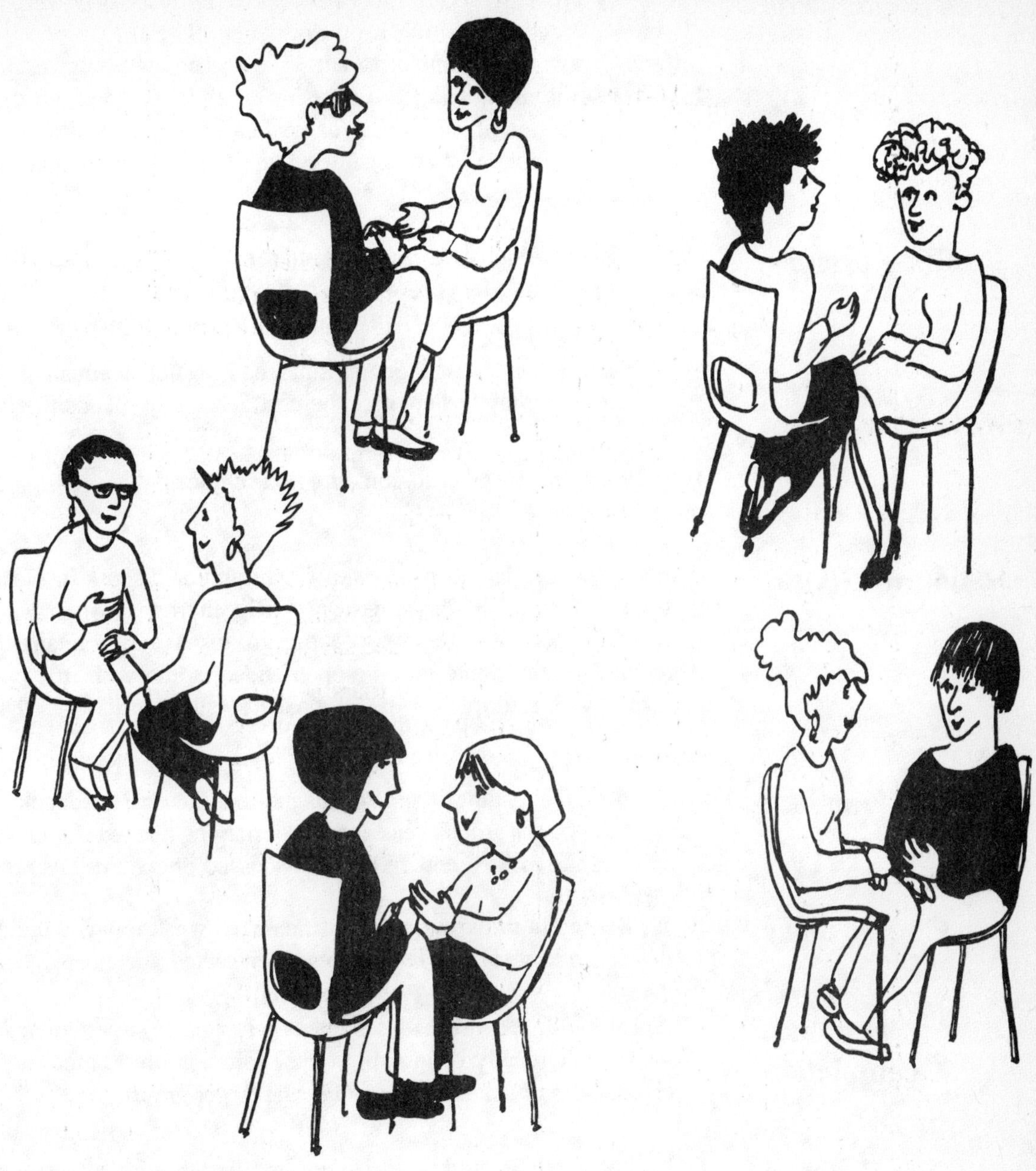

Sub-groups

Flip chart feedback

Record on the flip chart information/feedback from the group. Record exactly what each woman says, ie use the words spoken by each woman and not an interpretation of what she says. If you have to summarise, check that what you write is all right with the woman giving the feedback. As the group develops in confidence women may take turns in recording feedback.

Brainstorming

On a flip chart or board for all to see, list ideas from the group without alteration, comment, criticism or evaluation. The list can be used in several different ways: for example, to act as a trigger for group discussion, or as a basis for some more detailed discussion of an issue. Ideas on the chart can be sorted into different categories or ranked in order of importance. Missing aspects of a problem or issue can be identified before proceeding with further discussion or work.

Ranking exercise

Working individually or in sub-groups ask the women to put photographs, statements etc in order according to certain criteria:

* which they like the most/least
* which ones say most about an issue, eg injustice, inequality
* which ones they feel are most helpful, least helpful, positive/negative.

Bring the group together to compare their choices. A discussion may then take place based on the findings.

Questionnaire/Quiz

Allow a specific length of time to fill in and/or discuss it. General feedback may take place in the larger group. A flip chart may or may not be used to record feedback — it depends on the group. A questionnaire/quiz can have different formats. Some may be open-ended, some with true or false choices and some with multiple choice options. Reassure participants that this is not a test.

Handout

Allow time for reading it and for discussion. General feedback may then take place in the larger group. Pens and paper may be needed if individuals or small groups wish to make a note of points discussed or conclusions reached.

Course diary

Invite women in the group to take turns each week to write the diary, paste in copies of worksheets, and list activities completed.

Sentence completion

Circulate handouts with part-sentences referring to a particular issue or topic. Working individually or in sub-groups, complete the sentences. These can be shared in pairs or small groups and/or the larger group.

Lifeline

On a sheet of paper with a horizontal line drawn midway, ask each woman to list positive events in her life above the line and negative events below it as appropriate.

Debate

Participants prepare a short paper on a given motion either for or against. They present it in front of the group. After the arguments have been presented, the group may vote in favour of or against the motion.

Group project

Ask a small group, or a number of small groups, to find out certain information relating to a chosen topic. The small group may present it in a session to the rest of the group. Alternatively in a session, the large group may break into smaller groups to work together on specific tasks.

Collage

Invited speakers

Ask the speaker to give factual information on a particular subject matter, eg women and the law. They may also speak about their own personal experience of life, eg their experience of complementary medicine, depression, spirituality etc. The group may use the information in decision-making for themselves and in expanding their own knowledge and awareness of possibility and choice in daily living. Brief the speaker about the context into which the lecture is to be fitted. Give relevant background information on the group.

Personal history

Invite a woman to tell in a spontaneous way her life experience of a particular event. She may also relate it in story form, or verse. The sharing can be the basis of a discussion of the event and surrounding issues amongst the group.

Role-play

Introduce the role-play situation. Clarify the issues and roles. Encourage but do not pressurise women to participate. At the end of the role-play help each woman shed her role by asking her to focus on the here and now. During the role-play women may become embarrassed and slip out of their roles. Encourage them to stay in their role and explore the situation fully. Sometimes women may become very involved in the role-play and uncover strong emotions or buried pain which needs to be acknowledged. Some women may begin a role-play but stop if it gets too painful or difficult. This should be respected.

Drama

Choose a play written by a playwright or with the group devise your own. Decide on the theme, the roles, and the various parts. Then decide who will play the different parts, and where and when they will be performed. The group may also visit a theatre to see a play together.

Drawing/Collage

Give a sheet of paper with appropriate materials to each woman to make a drawing or a collage. Suggest a theme, an issue, or a topic on which the collage or drawing is based. On completion, share and discuss this in the group. (Too often we depend on verbal or written methods to explore issues and topics. It can be useful to introduce drawing or collage which allow more imaginative, less intellectualised responses to emerge. Unfortunately because many of us have been convinced in childhood that we are not creative, participants may feel intimidated if asked to draw or create a collage. It is important to encourage participants.)

Fantasy

Guided fantasy

Guided fantasies can be fun and relaxing. It is important to prepare the fantasy before the session. You can tape it and the group can listen to it or you can read it out. Do a brief relaxation exercise with the group. Tell them to close their eyes and imagine themselves in a safe place. Read out your guided fantasy very slowly, taking lots of time and pausing in between to allow women to use their imagination. Ask them to take a minute or two to open their eyes and be fully present in the room to bring them back to where they started from. Ask them to share as much or as little as they choose. It is very important to allow long pauses between each part of the fantasy.

Prose/Poems

Choose certain extracts from books, or certain poems to read in the group. Alternatively, ask the group to choose or to write their own.

Film/Video/Slides

They can be shown to the group by you or by an outsider with expertise in the appropriate technology. Or the group may visit a cinema together. View the film/video/slides prior to the session so that you are familiar with the content and issues raised. You may decide to supplement the material with handouts, questionnaires etc.

Music/Song

Choose appropriate songs and ask the group to make their own suggestions. Having explored an issue or topic, the group may write their own lyrics and music and perform it for other women's groups and/or for the community at large.

Photographs/ Cartoons/ Newspaper cuttings

Provide or ask women to collect newspaper/magazine cuttings on a particular subject matter. Photographs may be drawn from many sources — existing photo packs, personal photographs, photographs from newspapers/magazines. Members of the group may take photographs based on a particular issue. Cartoons can be collected from existing publications or drawn by participants. All can be used as discussion starters.

Graffiti sheet

Ask women to write their names on it, do drawings, symbols and/or write statements about positive changes and choices they are making in their personal lives and within the community.

Games

When the material in this workbook was being tested it was interspersed with introductory games, energisers, trust building games and relaxation exercises. Some of these are detailed below. When choosing games bear in mind the pace and tone of your session. For example, if you are doing very *heady* activities a fun game or a relaxation exercise would be appropriate. Details of useful publications for games etc are listed in the resources section (see pages 88-90).

Introductory games

Memorising names

Aim	To help group participants remember each other's names
Materials	None
Time	20 mins
Steps	The first woman introduces herself. The second woman introduces the first woman and then herself. The third woman introduces the first and second woman and then herself and so on. At the end of the exercise group participants are very familiar with the names of everyone in the group.
Credit	*Angela Mulligan*

Name game

Aim	To help participants relax. To get to know each other's names. To release shyness, anxiety and to have fun.
Materials	Soft cushion
Time	5 mins
Steps	Participants stand in a circle. Throw the cushion to a participant, she shouts her name as she catches it and throws it to someone else who in turn shouts out her name before passing it on. Encourage participants to throw a cushion round the group quickly to raise their energy and to release some laughter. It doesn't matter who throws to whom but it should make its way around the group several times. To finish ask one volunteer to go around the group and give everyone's name.
Credit	*Berni Divilly*

Name and action game

Aim	To relax group, to get to know each other's names and to have fun
Notes	Join in the exercise yourself. It is a fun game so help each other out if necessary.
Materials	Circle of chairs
Time	10 mins
Steps	Group sits in a circle. Each woman says her name and an action to go with it, eg *I'm Bernie and I scratch my arm*. The next person then introduces the first person and does the action, *this is Bernie and she scratches her arm* and then introduces herself and does another action, eg *and I'm Sandra and I jump up and down*. The third person then introduces Berni and scratches her arm, then introduces Sandra and jumps up and down and then introduces herself and does another action and so on until the last person has to try and remember all the names and has to do all the actions.
Credit	*Berny McMahon*

Name and adjective game

Aim	To get to know each other's names and to have fun
Materials	Circle of chairs, ball or soft item
Time	10 mins
Steps	Sit in a circle. Each woman says her name and a complimentary adjective that starts with the same letter as her name, eg *I'm Magnificent Mary, Brilliant Brigid* etc. Next get a ball or soft item and ask the participants to throw it to each other calling out the name and the adjective of the person they are throwing it to. The catcher throws to someone else and so on until everyone knows each other's names.
Credit	*Berny McMahon*

Energisers

Place change

Aim	To break the ice and to have fun
Note	Encourage the group to use their imaginations in making up instructions.
Materials	A circle of chairs
Time	10 mins
Steps	Group sits in a circle, the facilitator stands in the middle and gives instructions for changing places, eg *anybody wearing blue change places*. The facilitator tries to get a seat for herself and if she suceeds another woman will be left standing. She then gives an instruction and so the game continues.
Credit	*Berny McMahon*

Fun game

Aim	To have fun and to create a sense of group bonding
Materials	Circle of chairs
Time	10 mins
Steps	Sit in a large circle. The facilitator is without a chair and runs around the outside of the circle. She pretends to be some kind of locomotion or animal, complete with sound effects, eg plane, train,

sheep, cat, etc. As she goes around, she tips other members of the group and whoever is tipped must get up and follow her, doing what she does and making the same noises. The leader may *tip* as many members of the group as she wishes and then decide to call *halt*. When *halt* is called everyone tries to get a seat and someone else is left standing and she becomes some other kind of locomotion, or animal.

Credit *Berny McMahon*

Tails game

Aim To have fun

Materials 2 scarves

Time 10 mins

Steps Divide the group into two. Each sub-group stands in a chain holding on to each other's waists. The women at the end of each chain stick a scarf into their back pocket or waist band so it hangs down like a tail. Both chains start as far away as possible and the people at the front of each chain try to grab the tail of the other chain. If they succeed, the two tails people sit down and the next person in the chain takes the tail and so on until the last person is out or you have all had enough.

Credit *Berny McMahon*

Fruit game

Aim To help group participants to raise their energy level. As it is a fun game it also helps to lessen tension and to break down barriers.

Materials A rolled-up newspaper

Time 20 mins

Steps Each woman takes the name of a fruit and says it aloud to the group in turn. One woman stands in the centre. Someone shouts the name of a fruit other than their own or that of the woman standing in the centre. The woman in the centre must try to tap the head of the woman whose fruit has been named before that person has the opportunity to shout the name of another fruit. If she does she sits down and the other woman whose fruit has been named goes into the centre. The object of the game is to avoid being in the centre.

Credit *Angela Mulligan*

Balloon exercise

Aim To stretch and release tension

Notes Get the group to stand up and find enough space to comfortably move — then give the instructions. Join in the exercise yourself.

Materials None

Time 3 mins

Steps Pretend there is a balloon over your head. Now stretch up to reach it. As you move the balloon is floating around so you need to stretch higher — further — more — keep stretching. Now let go.

Credit *Berni Divilly*

Trust building games

A present

Aim To explore what participants would like to bring to the group. To create a feeling of having something to share

Notes The idea of a present is that we all can give something and we can use our imagination to create good feelings and nice things.

Materials None

Time 10 mins

Steps The facilitator asks the group to be quiet for a few minutes and to focus inside themselves. Then she asks them to focus on the group and to imagine a present they would like to make to the group, eg sunshine, humour, flowers .... Everyone shares her present.

Credit *Berni Divilly*

Graffiti sheet

Graffiti sheet

Aim To encourage group participants to publicly affirm themselves as well as ending the session or day on a positive note.

Materials A large cotton sheet and plenty of markers

Time 15-20 mins

Steps Facilitator or group member brings a large cotton sheet. At the end of a session or day each woman writes and/or draws on the sheet one or more affirming words/sentences/symbols affirming themselves. The group can agree where the graffiti sheet should be left. Preferably it should be displayed as a reminder of the day.

Relaxation exercises

Massage

Aim	To relax through being touched, to open up to giving and receiving with each other
Notes	Many feelings can be evoked by massage from being gently cared for to discomfort about our own bodies. Encourage participants to trust themselves to be able to touch somebody in a caring way and to be open to receive care from others and to allow themselves enjoy the experience. (The facilitator should demonstrate with a volunteer.) This can also be used as a trust building exercise.
Materials	None
Time	15 mins
Steps	Choose a partner. Sit on the floor or astride a chair with your back facing your partner. Take turns to give or receive a short back massage. Trust your own intuition as to what feels nice. You might like to gently massage up and down either side of the spine with a gentle fist .... or to give your partner's shoulder a knead .... or to firmly draw your hands down along either side of the spine in a long downward stroke .... Everyone knows how to massage; we just need to trust our ability to do it. When you are finished, place your hands quietly to rest on the other woman's shoulders so she knows the massage is over. Take your time moving away. Now change partners.
Credit	*Berni Divilly*

Relaxation and affirmation

Aim	To relax and release stress in the body. To create positive feelings about our sexuality
Notes	Use a full body relaxation exercise that you have experienced many times yourself. Write out the instructions for yourself so you don't forget it but don't bring these notes to the session. There is nothing worse than trying to relax to the crackle of paper.
Materials	Relaxation music (optional) tape recorder
Time	20 mins

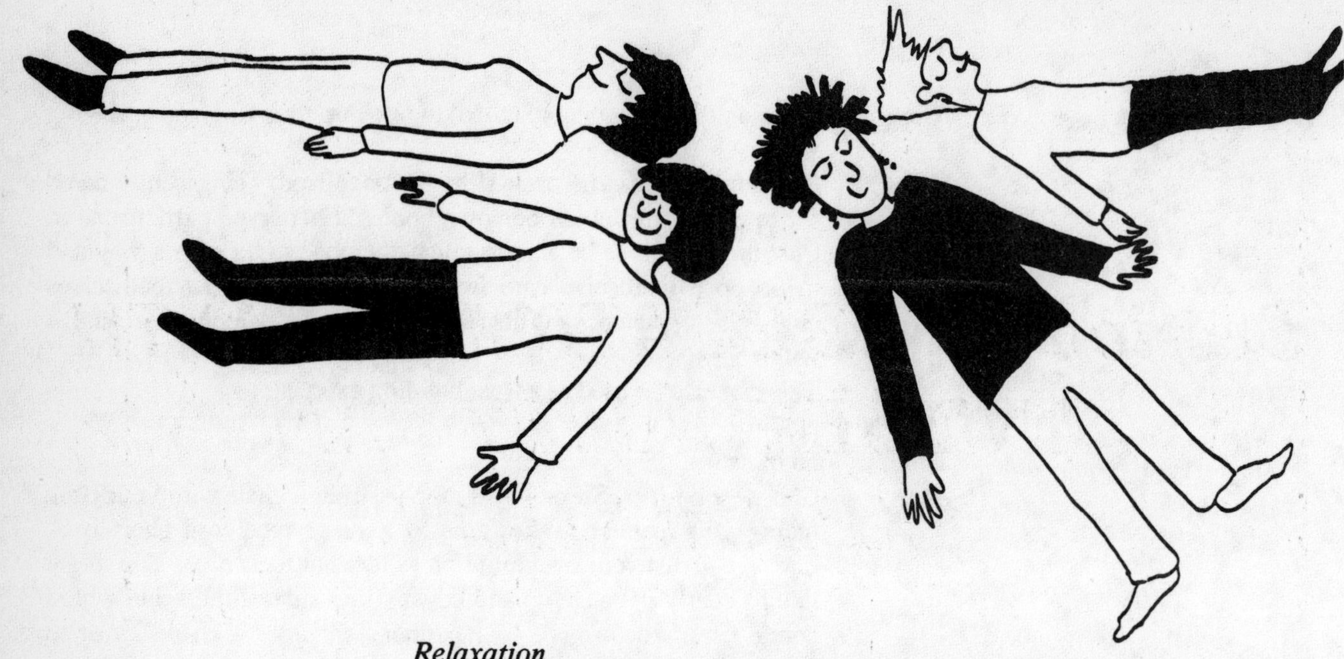

Relaxation

Steps	Before starting the relaxation exercise ask participants to think of a positive affirmation about their own sexuality. Ask them to structure it as a simple statement, eg *My body is pleasing and pleasurable to me*. Then lead the group step by step through a full body relaxation exercise. At the end of the relaxation, before opening their eyes or bringing their awareness back to the group .... ask them to repeat this affirmation to themselves silently three times.
Credit	*Berni Divilly*

Section D: *EDUCATION, HEALTH AND SEXUALITY – AN EXPLORATION*

Introduction to the Three Topics

The topics included in this workbook are education, health and sexuality. Each topic has a general aim and follows a pattern — experience, critical thinking, imagination and action. Any topic could be explored by a group using this model.

A number of activities are listed under each topic. They are designed in a sequence of steps. You can pick and choose from the suggested material and/or supplement it with other material drawn from your own resources depending on the interest of your group. When this material was used in workshops it was interspersed with games, relaxation exercises etc, as appropriate. Some of these are detailed earlier. See pages 46-52.

Each activity is laid out in the following format:

Aim An outline of the aim of the activity

Materials Details of any materials required to complete the activity are listed. The handouts for each activity are at the end of the relevant topic. They have been produced on A4 single pages for ease of reproduction. For activities which include a lot of writing or drawing it would be helpful to reproduce them on A3 (double A4) size paper. Many of the handouts may be written up on the flip chart and copied by participants.

Time Activities vary in the length of time they take. Take into account the number of women in the group and their previous experience when working out the approximate timing of each step. It is important to work at the pace of the group.

Activity Details of the activity and suggestions on how to work through it are listed under this heading. Details on the methods used in the activities are included in Active learning — see pages 40-46.

Many of the activities include working in small groups. This can help to increase involvement and participation. It allows those women who find it difficult to express themselves in the large group to do so within the safety of a small group. Vary the use of pairs and small groups.

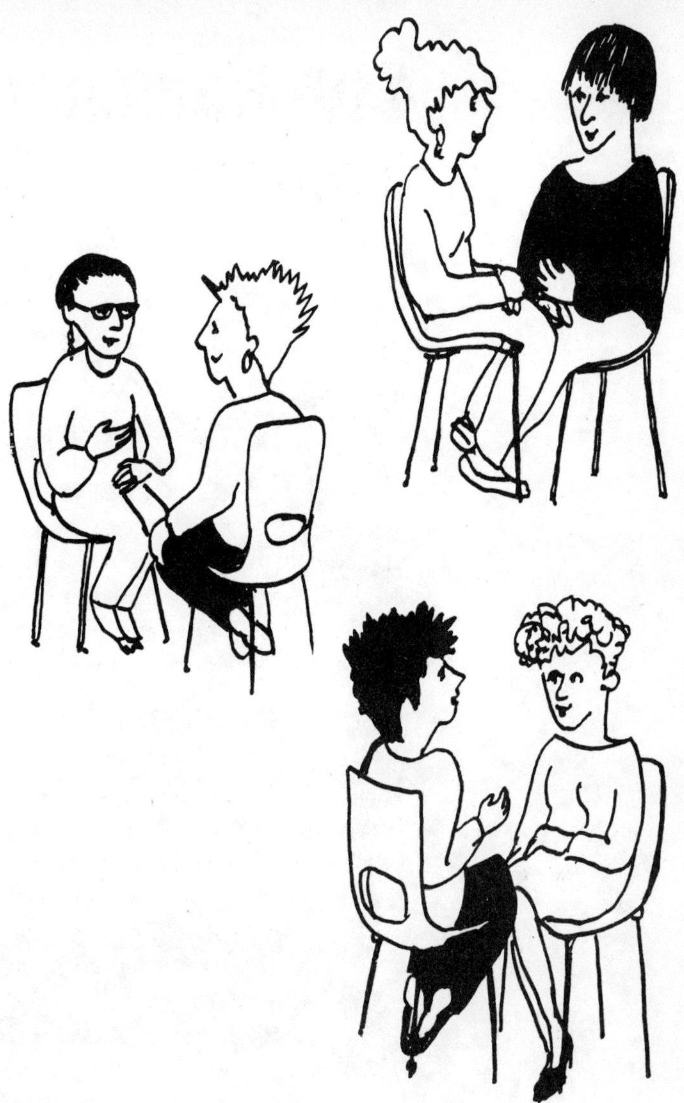

Working in pairs

It is suggested in some of the activities that participants record their thoughts. Be aware of the difficulties women may have with writing. Reassure participants that any writing is for their own personal use only.

Feedback Most of the activities end with feedback and discussion in the full group. We have included questions which might be useful in generating discussion. It is important to encourage all women to participate. Allow silences and time for thought. Encourage women to make their own connections and to come to their own conclusions. When taking feedback on the flip chart record exactly what each woman says, ie use key words spoken by each woman and not an interpretation of what she says. If you have to summarise check for accuracy with the woman giving feedback.

Notes Where appropriate we have included specific notes for the facilitator.

Credits We have credited the originators of material that we have adapted or used in this book. Material that we have originated or designed ourselves may be freely copied and adapted and we would ask you to credit us as appropriate.

Women and Education

Education plays a vital role in women's lives. School is often where we are taught to be *good little girls*. School also influences and limits subject choices and subsequent career options. Women's education can offer us an opportunity to develop self-confidence, to discover potential and to address inequalities.

In this section we explore our educational history and that of our mother and grandmother. We look at how girls are taught to behave. We also look at what attitudes and beliefs about women are transmitted through education and how these limit our opportunity to develop our potential. Finally we identify possibilities for action.

Experience

Tracing your history

Aim To explore your personal history of education and that of your mother and maternal grandmother and eldest daughter (if appropriate).

Materials A copy of handout (chart to be filled in — see page 64) for each participant preferably copied on A3 paper and markers. If it is not possible to use A3 paper (approximately twice the size of this page) ask participants to draw up their own chart based on the chart in the handout. Flip chart and paper for feedback.

Activity Begin by outlining the aim of this activity. Circulate handout and ask participants to fill it in individually. Then ask them to share in twos.

Feedback Questions for discussion in large group:

Are there similarities from generation to generation?
Are there differences from generation to generation?
How do you think the similarities and differences came about?
Are there any gaps in your knowledge about your family history?
How would you go about finding out more information?

Credit Adapted from National Union of Public Employees, Belfast unpublished activity *Dig where you stand*.

Note It is likely that there will be gaps in the information available about grandmothers and perhaps even mothers. This is an issue worth discussing in itself. Women's lives at both the public and private level are hidden from history and silenced. If there is time it would be interesting for the group to undertake as a project to get as much information about their mothers and grandmothers as they can and share it in a later session.

Girls should

Aim To examine differences in how girls and boys are *educated*

Materials A copy of handout (list of shoulds and should nots for girls and boys — see page 65) for each participant, and markers. Flip chart and paper for feedback.

Activity Begin by outlining the aim of this activity. Circulate handout and ask participants to fill it in individually.

Put up four sheets with the following headings:

Girls should
Boys should
Girls should not
Boys should not

Allow time for each participant to write one comment on each sheet.

Feedback Read aloud each sheet and ask for comments.

Questions for discussion:

What strikes you about the differences in expectations of girls and boys at school?

What impact does this schooling have on girls and on women?

Learning outside school

Aim To highlight the learning that takes place outside formal schooling.

Materials A copy of handout (series of questions — see page 66) for each participant, and markers. Flip chart and paper for feedback.

Activity Begin by outlining the aim of this activity. Circulate handout and ask participants to fill it in individually. Then ask them to share in twos.

Sharing in twos

Feedback In full group list all the factors which helped learning.

Critical thinking

Where do women figure?

Aim To highlight the subject choices of girls and the careers of women

Materials A copy of handout (questionnaire for Republic of Ireland or Northern Ireland as appropriate — see page 67, 68) for each participant, and pens or pencils.

Activity Begin by outlining the aim of this activity. Circulate questionnaires. Ask participants to complete on their own. Reassure them that this is not a test. Allow a specific length of time to fill in.

Correct Answers — Republic of Ireland

1. 52.1% of girls sat the Leaving Certificate in the 1987/88 exam year.

2. a. 39.3% of all those who sat higher Maths were girls.
   b. 24.7% of all those who sat Physics were girls.
   c. 64.7% of all those who sat Biology were girls.
   d. 2.6% of all those who sat Technical Drawing were girls.
   e. 91% of all those who sat Home Economics were girls.
   f. 34.5% of all those who sat Economics were girls.
   g. 64.6% of all those who sat Art (including craft) were girls.
3. 47.4% of first time entrants to third level courses in 1987/88 were women.
4. a. In the 1986 Census 64% of teachers were women.
   b. In the 1986 Census 23.5% of university professors/lecturers were women.
5. a. 98.4% of typists are women.
   b. 29% of medical doctors are women.
   c. 89.6% of nurses are women.
   d. 26% of judges, barristers, solicitors are women.
   e. 2.3% of engineers are women.
   f. 14.7% of accountants are women.
   g. 70.3% of bookkeepers are women.
   h. 23.7% of systems analysts/computer programmers are women.
   i. 74.9% of computing machine operators are women.

Correct Answers — Northern Ireland

1. a. 56.1% of o-level passes in Maths are gained by girls.
   b. 38.5% of o-level passes in Computer Science are gained by girls.
   c. 59% of o-level passes in Biology are gained by girls.
   d. 98.9% of o-level passes in Domestic Science are gained by girls.
   e. 21.6% of o-level passes in Geometrical Drawing are gained by girls.
   f. 23.9% of o-level passes in Physics are gained by girls.
2. 47% of university entrants are women.
3. 62% of the teaching profession is female.
4. 23% of teachers in higher education are women.
5. 150 of the 705 public representatives in the Department of Education (Northern Ireland) are women.
6. a. 99% of typists are women.
   b. 24% of medical and dental practitioners are women.
   c. 92% of nurses and nurse administrators are women.
   d. 12% of judges, barristers and solicitors are women.
   e. 9% of scientists, engineers and technicians are women.

Feedback — Questions for discussion in large group:

What did you learn from this activity?
Did anything surprise you about these current statistics?

Note — Statistics can be updated from the relevant sources.

Hidden agendas

Aim — To examine the thinking and attitudes behind education for women through reading quotations which range from the eighteenth century to the present

Materials — A copy of handout (quotes on education — see page 69) for each participant. Flip chart and paper for feedback.

Activity — Begin by outlining the aim of this activity. Circulate handout. In small groups each woman shares her response to the ideas in these quotations.

Feedback — Questions for discussion in large group:

What expectations for the education of women are evident in the quotations?
What were the ideas and attitudes informing your education?
Are there different ideas or attitudes informing education today? What are they?

Imagination

A school memory

Aim — To affirm women's creative skills through writing about a school memory: to offer an opportunity for quiet reflection on a school memory

Materials — Plenty of paper and pens

Activity — Begin by outlining the aim of the activity. Assure women that they can write — *you need to believe that as much as they do.* Ask women to recall a particular incident from school. For the next 15 minutes ask them to write about it in any way they like.

Feedback — Invite each participant to read aloud their writing.

Note — Some advice on a creative writing session.

* Offer a limited time in which to work — 15 mins is usually good, not long enough for high expectations and long enough to try something out.
* Tell women that they will be invited but not compelled to read out their work.
* Participate (write something yourself).
* Endeavour to get each woman to read what she has written — if she does, her pleasure and the group's appreciation will be worth it.
* Appreciate what each woman has done (a few lines are important to the woman who wrote them and deserve the attention of the group).

Action

Education and women's action

Aim — To identify what action women would like to take:
as individuals
as a group
within their communities.

Materials — A copy of handout (series of questions see page 70) for each participant. Flip chart and paper for feedback.

Activity Begin by outlining the aim of the activity. In small groups each woman shares her response to the questions in the handout.

Sharing in small groups

Feedback Questions for discussion in large group.

What are the actions women are considering taking?
What are the consequences of actions that women are considering?

Discuss the fears and obstacles to be faced in taking personal and group action.

Discuss the resources needed to take a particular action — a supportive environment, child care, transport, other group members, further information on opportunities, policies, funding, access etc.

What would be the first step?
What needs to be done next?

Women and Education — Experience Handout 1

Tracing your history

Fill in on your own with words, symbols, drawings etc.

	Born	Education	Work	Aspirations	Further education and training
Daughter					
Self					
Mother					
Maternal grandmother					

Permission to photocopy

Women and Education — Experience Handout 2

Girls Should Fill in on your own

At school I learned that girls should:	
At school I learned that girls should not:	
At school I learned that boys should:	
At school I learned that boys should not:	

Permission to photocopy

Women and Education — Experience Handout 3

Learning outside school

Think of something you learned outside of school. It has to be something you remember learning, something that is important to you.

* Think carefully about how you learned it.

* Why did you learn it?

* Who helped you learn it?

* What was the relationship between you and the person who helped?

* How did you learn it?

* Did anything make the learning easier?

Permission to photocopy

Women and Education — Critical Thinking Handout 1

Where do women figure? Republic of Ireland

1. What percentage of girls sat the Leaving Certificate in the 1987/88 exam year?

   34.5% 52.1% 56.7%

2. What percentage of all those who sat the following subjects were girls?

a.	Maths-higher	23.3%	48.6%	39.3%
b.	Physics	24.7%	56.5%	31.9%
c.	Biology	41.2%	64.7%	27.4%
d.	Tech Draw	12.5%	16.5%	2.6%
e.	Home Econ	59%	91%	80%
f.	Economics	24.3%	34.5%	59.1%
g.	Art (inc. craft)	80.7%	20.3%	64.6%

Department of Education 1987/88

3. What percentage of first time entrants to third level courses in 1987/88 were women?

   47.45% 36.5% 59.9%

4. In the 1986 Census what percentage were women?

   a. teachers 33% 56% 64%

   b. university professors/lecturers

   32.8% 49.4% 23.5%

5. Tick which you think is correct.

a.	64.3%	87.8%	98.4%	of typists are women
b.	17%	29%	39%	of medical doctors are women
c.	89.6%	75.2%	96.1%	of nurses are women
d.	14%	26%	42%	of judges, barristers, solicitors are women
e.	7.6%	2.3%	12.4%	of engineers are women
f.	23.8%	5.6%	14.7%	of accountants are women
g.	70.3%	89.9%	53.9%	of bookkeepers are women
h	16.7%	23.7%	28.2%	of systems analysts/ computer programmers are women
i.	74.9%	53.6%	28.9%	of computing machine operators are women

1986 Census

Permission to photocopy

Women and Education — Critical Thinking Handout 2

Where do women figure? Northern Ireland

1. What percentage of o-level passes are gained by girls?

a.	Maths	28.4%	56.1%	47.6%
b.	Computer Science	38.5%	16.3%	24.4%
c.	Biology	74.6%	48.3%	59.0%
d.	Domestic Science	62.7%	98.9%	57.2%
e.	Geometrical Drawing	21.6%	13.5%	2.4%
f.	Physics	34.4%	18.7%	23.9%

2. What percentage of university entrants are women?
   32% 47% 62%

3. What percentage of the teaching profession is female?
   42% 52% 62%

4. What percentage of teachers in higher education are women?
   23% 33% 43%

5. There are 705 public representatives in the Department of Education (Northern Ireland). How many of these do you think are women?
   15% 25% 35%

6. Tick which you think is correct:
   a. 99% 87% 73% of typists are women
   b. 16% 24% 38% of medical and dental practitioners are women
   c. 76% 92% 84% of nurses and nurse administrators are women
   d. 27% 8% 12% of judges, barristers and solicitors are women
   e. 9% 16% 22% of scientists, engineers and technicians are women

Statistics taken from 'Where do Women Figure?' Equal Opportunities Commission, Northern Ireland.

Permission to photocopy

Women and Education — Critical Thinking Handout 3

Hidden agendas

The whole education of women ought to be relative to men; to please them, to be useful to them, to make themselves loved and honoured by them, to educate them when young, to care for them when grown, to counsel them, to console them and to make life sweet and agreeable to them. These are the duties of women at all times.

Jean-Jacques Rousseau 1762

A good girl is tidy. A good girl makes herself pretty. A good girl is polite, docile, demure, submissive, passive, gentle, caring, giving, dependent, chaste. She stays out of trouble. Fighting is for boys, not for girls. Learn these lessons well and you will get a gold star: a boy-friend, a ring, a husband, social approval.

Beale, J. *Women in Ireland, Voices of Change*
London and Dublin, Gill and MacMillan, 1986, p 130.

.... separate arrangements in movement training may be made for boys and girls. Boys can now acquire skills and techniques and girls often become more aware of style and grace .... (movement) .... while a large number of songs are suited to boys, for example, martial, gay, humorous, rhythmic airs. Others are more suited to girls, for example, lullabies, spinning songs, songs tender in content and expression.

1971 *Primary School Curriculum*
Teachers' Handbook Part 2 — still in use.

The current version of the stereotypes of what it is to be a woman says that women .... are best fulfilled personally as individual human beings and make their best contribution to society by life as wife and mother .... This model influences the educational experience of girls and women in a number of ways. It determines the areas of human knowledge made available to and seen as suitable for girls and women. It affects the encouragement and discouragement given to girls to study various subjects. It influences the choices girls themselves make and the degrees of self-confidence they bring to the subjects chosen.

Cullen, Mary, *Girls Don't Do Honours,* page 136, WEB, Dublin 1987.

Permission to photocopy

Women and Education — Action Handout

Education and women's action

* What would you like to change?
  for yourself
  for your group
  in your community

* What opportunities are there?

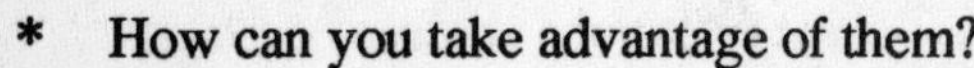

* How can you take advantage of them?

* What obstacles are in your way?

* How can they be overcome?

* Have you taken any action already?

* What will it mean for you?

* What opportunities and obstacles present themselves?

Permission to photocopy

Women and Health

Health issues regularly emerge in women's groups as a topic for lively discussion. Common experiences both positive and negative are explored and concerns are highlighted. Until recently the health care system did not address the specific needs of women. Changes are now being implemented mainly as a result of pressure from women and from concerned individuals working in health education and service provision. To maintain this impetus for change women need to clarify their concerns and assert their priorities.

In this section we explore individual experience, consider the factors which affect women's health, and examine possibilities for change and action.

Experience

Personal history of health

Aim To recall our personal experience of mental and physical health

Materials A copy of handout (image of woman's body — see page 76) for each participant, and plenty of colourful markers

Activity Begin by outlining the aim of this activity. Circulate handout and ask participants to mark in their personal history of health both as a girl and as a woman. Encourage participants to include mental as well as physical health in the handout. Words, symbols or drawings can be used. Ask them to share in twos. In testing this activity we found that women needed time to share their experiences before moving on.

Feedback Each participant shares one experience *briefly* in large group.

Good and bad experiences

Aim To examine what contributes to a good and a bad experience of health care

Materials Pen and paper if desirable. Flip chart and paper for feedback.

Activity Begin by outlining the aim of this activity. Working on their own, ask participants to consider one good and one bad experience of where they sought help with a health problem. Working in twos, ask them to identify their good and bad experiences.

Feedback In large group brainstorm on what contributes to good and bad experiences — record these on two separate sheets.
Questions for discussion in large group:

What are your priorities when you visit a health practitioner?
Are they understood by her or him?
What can you do when you are not satisfied?

Sources of help		
	Aim	To examine where we have gone for help with health problems.
	Materials	Paper and pens if appropriate. Flip chart and paper for feedback.
	Activity	Begin by outlining the aim of this activity. Working on their own, ask participants to think about the people and places they approached for help.
	Feedback	In large group list all people and places they approached for help. Questions for discussion in the large group: What strikes you about this feedback? Any patterns/similarities/differences? Are there any other forms of help that are not listed? (Facilitator's own information or experience can be added here if appropriate.) What limits our choice in health care?

Critical thinking

Snakes and ladders		
	Aim	To highlight the factors that affect women's health and that limit their options when deciding what action to take.

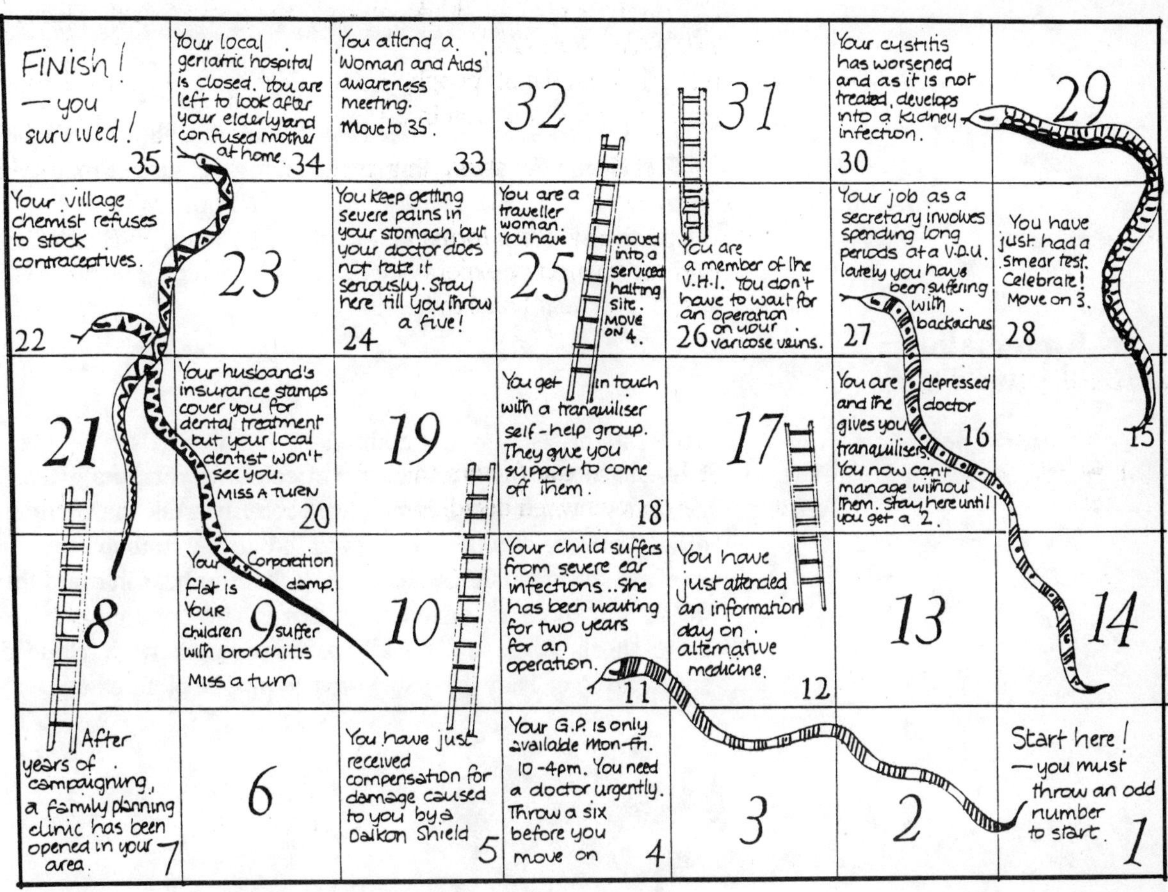

Snakes and ladders

Materials A copy of the handout (snakes and ladders — see page 77) for each participant, counters and dice. Flip chart and paper for feedback.

Activity Begin by outlining the aim of this activity. Ask participants to play the game in twos, threes or fours. Allow sufficient time. Ask participants to remain in their small groups and answer the following questions:

How did you feel when playing this game?

How does this game compare to your own experience?

Feedback Questions about the healthcare system for discussion in the large group:

Does it serve women's needs?

What assumptions are made about women?
Who benefits from it?
What values and priorities are reflected in the healthcare system?

Credit: Snakes and Ladders adapted from *Women and Health. Activities and Materials for use in Women's Health Courses and Discussion Groups*. Published by Workers' Educational Association (North West District)/Health Education Council 1986. Available from WEA North Western District, Crawford House, Precinct Centre, Oxford Road, Manchester M13 9GH or WEA, Publications Department, 9 Upper Berkeley Street, London W1H 8BY. Price £5 + £1.50 p&p.

Imagination

Community needs

Aim: To creatively explore our community health needs

Materials: Large sheets of paper and plenty of colourful markers

Activity: Begin by outlining the aim of this activity. Ask the participants to draw a picture of what they would like to see in their community to improve the standard of health. Ask them to bear in mind their own needs and those of different groups in the community. Distribute large sheets of paper and ask participants to work alone or with someone else. They can use words, symbols, pictures etc.

Working in pairs

Working in pairs, ask participants to rank the needs of their community in order of priority.
Feedback in full group and list the top priority for each pair.
It may be useful to agree 3 or 4 priorities for action which can then be used in the following activity.

Action

The obstacle race

Aim	To clarify what is helping or hindering us and what action we can take to achieve our goal once it has been decided upon.
Note	In the previous activity we identified and ranked some of our community health needs. If you have not completed the above activity it will be necessary to brainstorm on current health needs and community priorities.
Materials	Paper, markers and tape/blue-tack
Activity	Begin by outlining the aim of this activity. Break into small groups and ask each group to choose a specific objective which they would like to achieve. Ask them to list all (a) the obstacles that would hinder them in achieving their aim; and (b) the factors that would help them. Next they choose an obstacle to overcome and identify ways in which this could be done. Finally they agree on a helping factor and decide on how it can be best used to achieve their aim.
Feedback	Invite each group to present their work for discussion in the large group.

Women and Health — Experience Handout

Personal history of health (Image of woman's body)

Mark out your personal history of mental and physical health both as a girl and as a woman — you can use words, symbols or drawings.

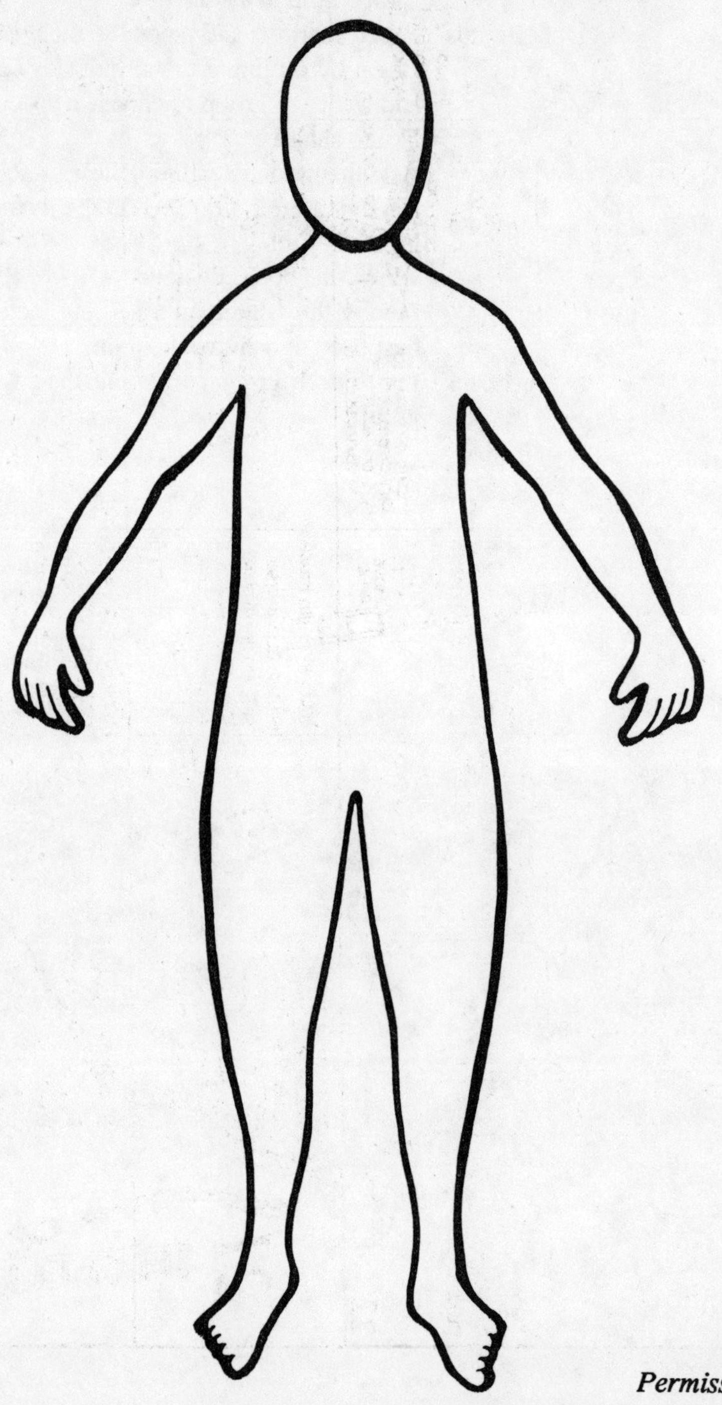

Permission to photocopy

Women and Health — Critical Thinking Handout

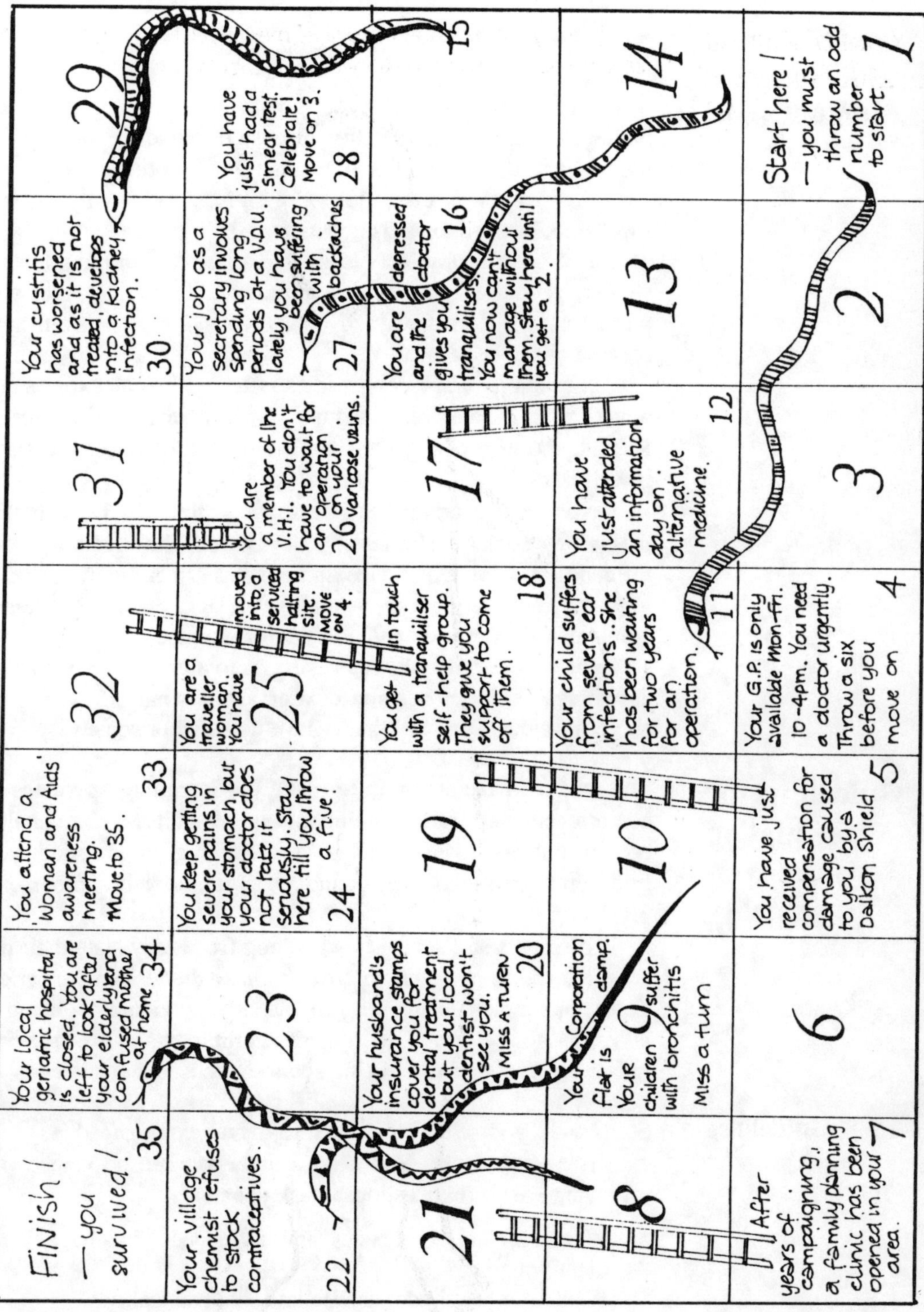

Permission to photocopy

Women and Sexuality

Introduction

Sexuality is about being in touch with our feelings, and being aware of our bodies. We all have a sexuality, a sense of ourselves as sexual persons. We all have physical and emotional needs. Our emotional needs can be met in a variety of ways. We can get a lot of satisfaction from good friendships, being supported, listened to, and encouraged.

Our needs for physical closeness can be met through hugs and cuddles — we may get these from friends, children and family. We may also enjoy sensual pleasures in different ways by ourselves — a walk by the sea, a bath with scented oils, a tasty meal.

Our sexuality embraces a wide spectrum. We can express ourselves through a variety of sexual relationships — these may be heterosexual, bi-sexual, lesbian, and may change over the course of our lives. We may also choose to be celibate.

Sexuality is a private and personal matter. At the same time sexuality is defined by society. The family, the church, the media and our education all influence how we experience and express our sexuality. These social institutions together define our sexuality for us. Such definitions can result in ambivalence, confusion and conflict for women.

Exploring our sexuality can bring us to a greater understanding of ourselves as women. We can become clearer about what we want for ourselves, the choices we make and the changes we want in our society.

Guidelines for facilitating workshops on sexuality

The role of a facilitator is to make the learning experience easy. When we come together to learn more about our sexuality, we are challenging the very core of our oppression. This is very exciting empowering work. And it may bring up strong emotions, including anger, anxiety, enjoyment, fear, fun and grief.

Participants at a sexuality workshop frequently state their need to feel safe, accepted and to have fun, in order to make the learning experience a good one. Their fears include being judged, misunderstood and not being able to speak. It is useful to be aware that many participants will have known only too intimately experiences of being silenced, abused and coerced.

Guidelines

Start with yourself. You need to have experienced as a participant any exercises you choose. You need to have worked on your own sexuality. The following are useful questions to ask yourself.

* What are the experiences and influences that have shaped my sexual identity to date?
* What are my attitudes and beliefs about sexuality?
* How do I imagine these may be different from those of other women?

* How do I feel about different attitudes, beliefs and choices?
* What would be easy to reveal about myself?
* What would be difficult?
* What aspects of sexuality might I have difficulty with?
* What experiences/support can I draw on in preparation for work on sexuality?
* How might my answer to the above questions affect the way I facilitate?

If possible co-facilitate sexuality workshops. It is good to have the help of another facilitator in running and assessing the workshops. It increases the support available for both facilitators and participants.

Experience

Collage on sexual messages

Aim — To explore the messages about sexuality that influence our ideas and beliefs

Materials — Plenty of women's magazines, preferably a mix of mainstream and feminist, large sheets of paper, scissors, glue and markers. Flip chart and paper for feedback

Activity — Begin by introducing the aim of the activity. Ask each participant to take a large sheet of paper, scissors, markers and glue. From the pile of magazines ask them to cut out and make a collage of images that represent messages they have received about sexuality.

Collage

Sexual labels word association

Aim To become aware of our uncensored thoughts about some of the labels associated with sexual choices

Materials A copy of handout for each participant, paper and plenty of markers

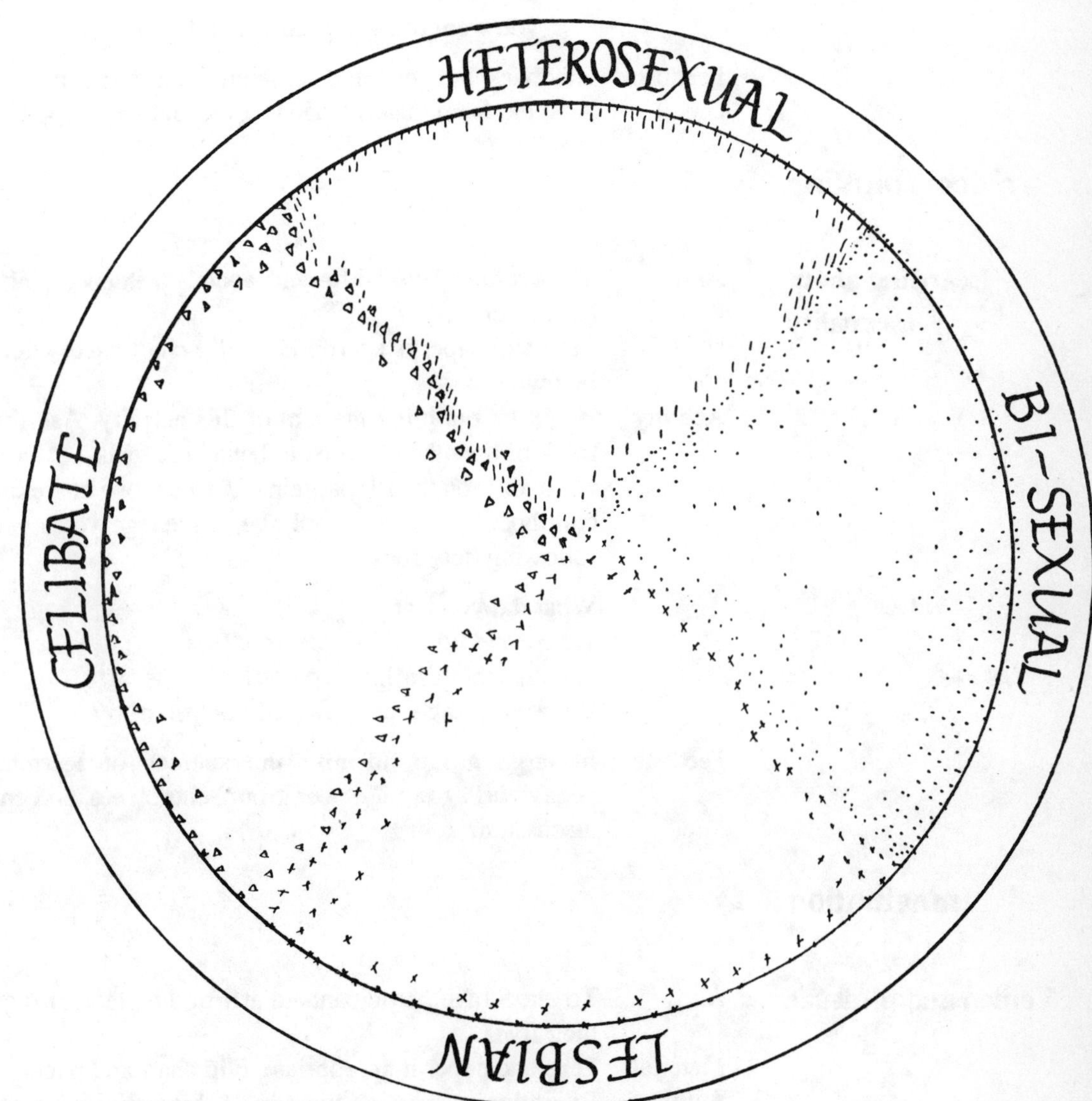

Sexuality circle

Activity Begin by outlining the aim of this activity. Circulate handout. On their own, ask participants to write down all the words, names etc, they associate with each label in the corresponding space in the circle. When they have finished ask them to draw an image of what comes to mind for each of these labels.

In pairs, ask participants to discuss the following questions:

Has anything come up that
surprised you?
challenged you?
pleased you?
you were uncomfortable with?

Feedback — Feedback and general discussion in large group.
Credit — Adapted from material used by the Galway Rape Crisis Centre

Critical thinking

Learning about sexuality

Aim — To explore how different social influences affect our sexual behaviour

Materials — Pens and paper if appropriate. Flip chart sheet with questions listed below

Activity — Begin by outlining the aim of this activity. Ask the participants to think of how they learned to behave as girls.
In small groups, ask participants to choose one example from early childhood, primary school age or teenage years and to address the following questions:

What did you learn?
Where and how did you learn it?
Who taught or influenced you?
Whose messages are powerful for you now?

Feedback — In large group, identify the sources of learning about sexual behaviour, eg family, peer group, church etc, and encourage general discussion.

Imagination

Women and pleasure

Aim — To encourage participants to affirm the place of pleasure and fun in their lives

Materials — Pens and paper if appropriate. Flip chart and paper for feedback

Activity — Begin by introducing the aim of this activity. In small groups, ask participants to describe types of sensual pleasure that they enjoy, eg a warm bath, a massage, a nice meal, a cuddle.

Feedback — In the large group ask each woman to contribute one sensual pleasure and list these on the flip chart.
In small groups, plan a women's pleasure day using this list.
In full group share different plans.

Action

Positive aspects of being a woman

Aim
To encourage women to think positively about how they see themselves.

Materials
Flip chart sheet with questions listed below.

Activity
Begin by introducing the aim of the activity. In small groups ask participants to discuss:

What are the positive aspects of being a woman?
How can we maximise this potential?
Where can we start?

Feedback
Question for discussion in large group:

What action can you take
for youself?
with other women?
to challenge society's ideas about women's sexuality?

Women and Sexuality — Experience Handout

Sexual labels word association

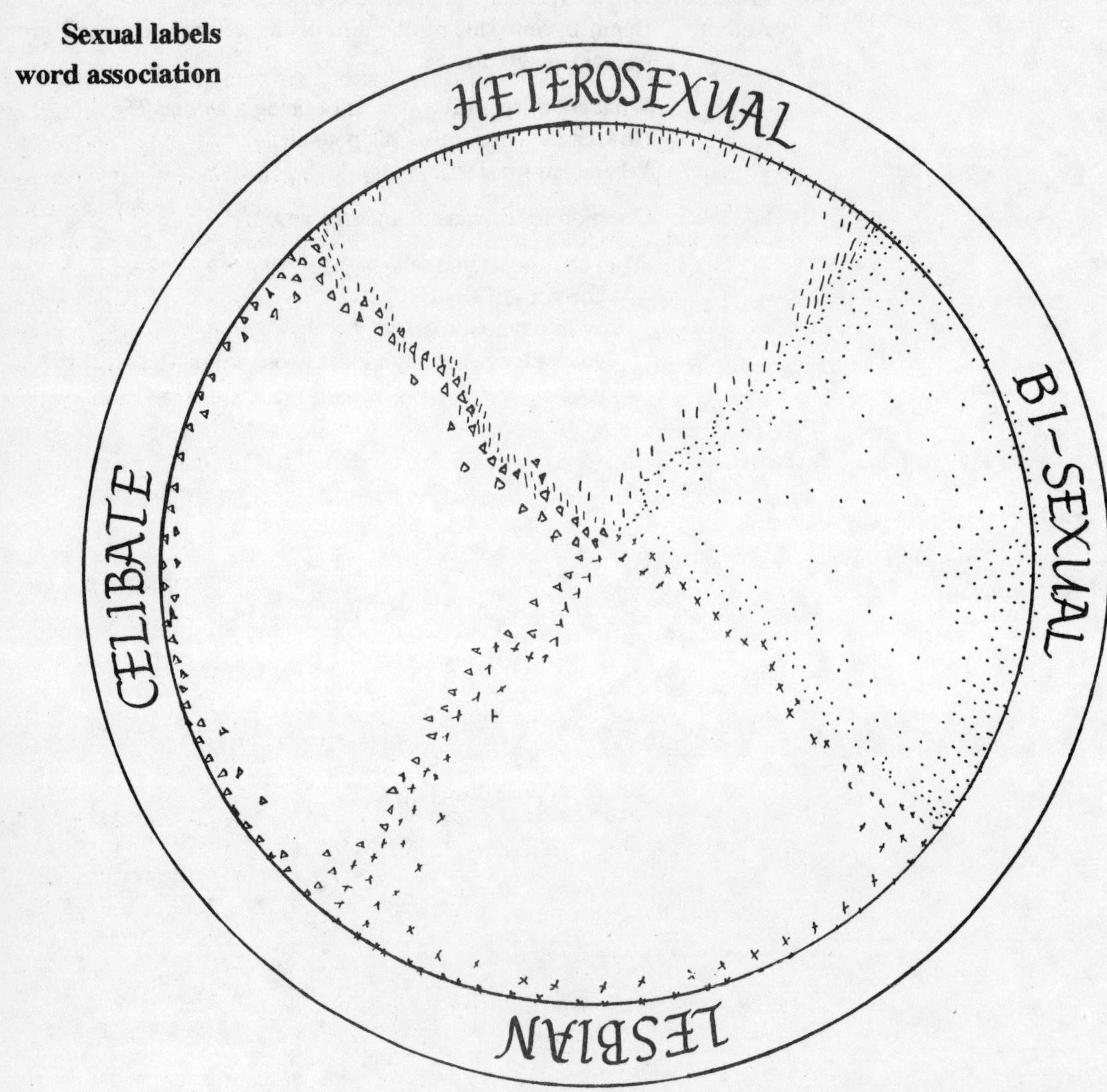

* Write down all words, names etc, you associate with each label in the corresponding space in the circle.
* On the back of the handout draw an image of what comes to mind for each of these labels.

Permission to photocopy

Building Blocks

If you have followed the activities listed under each topic you will be familiar with the spiral model of learning. You may wish to plan other activities for your group depending on the time available. If you wanted to encourage action on health you could inititate discussion on practical ways women can look after their health, eg cervical smear test (perhaps those women who have neglected this could arrange to go together). Where areas of interest are shared group members could take responsibility to find people locally who might talk about their area of expertise/interest: acupuncture, massage, homoepathy etc. You could also carry out a local survey of services available, eg from social services, voluntary agencies, and community organisations. Alternatively you could set up a questions and answers session where local administrators, eg chief executive officer of health board, councillors, politicians, programme manager, director of community care etc attend a public session to answer questions from the audience on health policy and provision.

Other topics

Brainstorming

If you wanted to explore another topic, for example, work, you could begin by exploring women's experience of work. You could use the *Dig Where You Stand* activity altering the headings to suit. Next examine where women are in the labour force and what are their pay and conditions of employment. Consider paid and unpaid work and who benefits. Under Imagination you could have a fantasy on different ways of organising work and types of working environments. Alternatively you could select some creative writing and either read them aloud, or invite participants to do so, following with discussion. For Action you could identify women's training needs or make a skills inventory and see where these could be used.

Section E: RESOURCES

Useful Publications

Bailey, Kay; Mary Connolly; Marie McIntyre and Christine Murray, *Information Pack for Daytime Adult Education Groups*, Dublin, AONTAS, National Association for Adult Education, 22 Earlsfort Terrace, Dublin 2, 1990.

Bassett, Maureen; Elaine Kelly Conroy; Michael Kenny and Colm Regan, *Justice in Action Project*, Dublin, A Joint Development Education Programme, Trócaire, 169 Booterstown Avenue, Co. Dublin, and Macra na Feirme, Irish Farm Centre, Bluebell, Dublin 12, £2.00.

McDonagh, Michael; Ray Mooney; Geraldine Murphy; Paul Noonan and PJ O'Reilly, *Pride and Prejudice: the case of the Travellers*, Navan Travellers Committee, 1988 available from Trócaire, 12 Cathedral Street, Dublin 1, £2.00.

Schonveld, Jane, *Assertiveness Workshops: A Guide for Group Leaders*, copies available from Community Education Office, The James Young High School, Quentin Rise, Dedridge, Livingston, West Lothian, Scotland EH54 6 NG, 1987, £5.00.

Developed by tutors of *NOW* and *Carry on Learning* courses in Scotland, *Getting Started: a basic education pack for tutors/organisers working with women in informal learning groups*, Workers' Educational Association, Temple House, 9 Upper Berkeley Street, London WIH 8BY, 1982, £4.95.

Workers' Education Association, North Western District/Health Education Council, *Women and Health. Activities & Materials for use in Women's Health Courses and Discussion Groups*, WEA Publications Department, 9 Upper Berkeley Street, London W1H 8BY at £5 plus £1.50 p & p.

Hope, Anne and Sally Timmel, *Training for Transformation. A Handbook for Community Workers. Books 1, 2, and 3*, Mambo Press, Gweru, Zimbabwe, 1987, available from Trócaire, 12 Cathedral Street, Dublin 1, £10.00 for full set.

The Clarity Collective, *Taught not Caught: strategies for sex education*, published by Learning Development Aids, Wisbeck, Cambs. England, 1985, £14.50, available from IFPA Education Resource Centre, Lr. Ormond Quay, Dublin.

Brandes, Donna and H Phillips, *Gamesters Handbook 1 & 2*, (Stanley Thornes Publishers), Hutchinson Publishers Group Limited, 1977. £9.75 each.

Winners All, Co-operative Games for all Ages, London, Pax Christi, St. Francis of Assisi Centre, Pottery Lane, London W11 4NG, 1980, £1.30 available from Trócaire, 12 Cathedral Street, Dublin 1.

Kiernan, Giliofa, *New Club Games*, Dublin, National Youth Federation, 20 Lower Dominick Street, Dublin 1, 1989. £3.75.

Ernst, Sheila and Lucy Goodison, *In Our Own Hands. A Book of Self Help Therapy*, London: The Women's Press, 1981.

Some books you might find useful in relation to the three topics:

Inglis, Tom and Maureen Bassett, *Live and Learn: Day-time Adult Education in Coolock*, Dublin, AONTAS, 1988.

Daly, Mary, *Women and Poverty*, Dublin, Attic Press, 1989.

Steiner-Scott, Liz (ed) *Personally Speaking — Women's Thoughts on Women's Issues*, Dublin, Attic Press, 1985.

Thompson, Jane, *Learning Liberation — Women's Response to Men's Education*, Croom Helm, 1983.

Spender, Dale and Sarah E, *Learning to Lose: Sexism and Education*, The Women's Press, 1980.

Cullen, Mary, *Girls Don't Do Honours*, Dublin, WEB, 1987.

Beale, Jenny, *Women in Ireland, Voices of Change*, London, MacMillan and Dublin, Gill & Macmillan, 1986.

Bristol Women's Studies Group, *Half the Sky: an introduction to women's studies*, Virago, 1979.

Hughes, M and M Kennedy, *New Futures: Changing Women's Education*, Routledge & Kegan Paul, 1985.

Roper, Anne, *Woman to Woman: A Health Care Handbook and Directory for Women*, Dublin, Attic Press, 1986.

Schaeff, Anne Wilson, *When Society becomes an Addict*, Harper and Row, 1987.

Ehrenreich, Barbara and Deirdre English, *For her own good — 150 years of experts' advice to women*, London, Pluto, 1979.

Coward, Rosyland, *Female Desire*, Paladin, 1984.

Edited by Feminist Review, *Sexuality: A Reader*, Virago, 1987.

Kitzinger, Sheila, *Women's Experience of Sex*, London, Penguin, 1985.

Dublin Lesbian and Gay Men's Collective, *Out for Ourselves*, Dublin, Women's Community Press, 1986.

Loulan, Jo Ann, *Lesbian Sex*, San Francisco, Spinster's Ink, 1984.

Useful Addresses

Republic of Ireland

AONTAS, National Association of Adult Education, 22 Earlsfort Terrace, Dublin 2. Telephone 754121/754122.

National Adult Literacy Agency, 8 Gardiner Place, Dublin 1. Telephone 787205.

Council for the Status of Women, 64 Lr. Mount Street, Dublin 2. Telephone 615268.

Employment Equality Agency, 36 Upper Mount Street, Dublin 4. Telephone 605966.

Combat Poverty Agency, 8 Charlemont Street, Dublin 8. Telephone 783355.

CAFE (Creative Activity for Everyone) C/o City Centre, 23-25 Moss Street, Dublin 2. Telephone 770330.

Women's Education Project, 129 University Street, Belfast BT7 1HP. Telephone 230212.

Northern Ireland

Workers' Education Association, 1 Fitzwilliam Street, Belfast 7. Telephone 329718.

Equal Opportunities Commission for Northern Ireland, Chamber of Commerce House, 22 Great Victoria Street, Belfast BT2 7BA. Telephone 242752.

Index

H

I

L

M

N

O

P

Q

R

S

T

U

V

W